The Wild Coast

THE
WILD
COAST

* * * * * * *

Exploring the Natural Attractions
of the Mid-Atlantic

CURTIS J. BADGER

ILLUSTRATIONS BY MARY ANN CLARKE

University of Virginia Press

Charlottesville and London

University of Virginia Press
© 2005 by Curtis J. Badger
All rights reserved
Printed in the United States of America on acid-free paper

First published 2005

1 3 5 7 9 8 6 4 2

LIBRARY OF CONGRESS CATALOGING-IN-PUBLICATION DATA
Badger, Curtis J.
The wild coast : exploring the natural attractions of the
Mid-Atlantic / Curtis J. Badger; illustrations by Mary Ann Clarke.
p.   cm.
ISBN 0-8139-2333-6 (pbk. : alk. paper)
1. Natural history–Atlantic Coast (Middle Atlantic
States)–Guidebooks. 2. Atlantic Coast (Middle Atlantic
States)–Guidebooks. I. Title.
QH104.5.M45B33 2005
508.75–dc22   2004020121

To Anna and Hallett Badger,
who did their best to raise me up right

Contents

Acknowledgments

THANKS GO FIRST OF ALL TO MY WIFE, LYNN, AND SON, TOM, who accompanied me on many of the trips described here. Their companionship made my journeys infinitely more enjoyable. In compiling a book such as this, I find that I am often, in the words of Blanche DuBois in *A Streetcar Named Desire*, dependent upon the kindness of strangers. The fulfilling thing is that once the book is completed, the strangers often are no longer strangers, but friends.

Making lists is a dangerous thing, because I will inevitably leave out the name of someone who helped me greatly, and as soon as the book is off the press I will recall that name and feel very embarrassed about my omission. And so with that caveat, let us begin the salutes, working our way generally from north to south.

Through his writings and stories, John Terres, a New Jersey native, writer, and ornithologist, introduced me to Island Beach long before I ever set foot there. The folks at the New Jersey chapter of the Nature Conservancy introduced me to their preserves in the Cape May area and along the Delaware bayshore. The staffs of various tourism offices provided a great deal of guidance and information.

On the inland bays of Delaware, I spent several enjoyable days aboard the *Sand Dollar* with Captain Larry Karpinski and naturalists Kristel Sharman and Colleen Schilly. The staff at Cape Henlopen State Park sent me in search of snowy owls and snow buntings. Ed Lewandowski introduced me to the James Farm, an educational preserve managed by the Delaware Center for the Inland Bays.

Bill Bostian of the Nature Conservancy guided me through the Nassawango Creek Preserve, one of the largest in Maryland. Captains Buddy Harrison and Allen Bryan of Tilghman Island fed Lynn and me oysters and showed us how to catch rockfish. On Smith Island, LeRoy Friesen and Sharryl Lindberg fed us rockfish and fried soft crabs at the Inn of Silent Music in the idyllic village of Tylerton. Waverly Evans, who grew up in Tylerton, showed us the natural attractions of the island, complete with historical commentary.

In Virginia I have long enjoyed a close relationship with the staff of the Virginia Coast Reserve and the state chapter of the Nature Conservancy. Many of the staff members helped in numerous ways. Mary Kathryn van Eerden introduced Lynn and Tom and me to the North Landing River, and her husband, Brian, invited us to come along on a red-cockaded woodpecker relocation program in the Green Sea, that vast area of coastal wilderness that once included the Great Dismal Swamp and much of southeast Virginia and northeast North Carolina.

Barbara and Wilson Snowden of Currituck shared with me the history and culture of waterfowl hunting in coastal North Carolina. Tillman Merrell, a hunting guide during the great days of waterfowling on Currituck Sound, explained the use of live decoys. Tom Fotti, a contemporary guide who paddles a sea kayak instead of a duck boat, showed me around Roanoke Island by water. John Fussell, a birding expert and author of birding guides, showed me the birds of the Crystal Coast. Bouty Baldridge, the Cape Fear river keeper, shared with me his vision for the future of this wild place. Others helped with guidance and introductions. These include Janis Williams of the Crystal Coast, who arranged numerous trips for me, as did Connie Nelson of the Cape Fear Coast and Quinn Capps of the Outer Banks. Many thanks to all of you.

Introduction

THIS IS A BOOK FOR PEOPLE WHO LIKE TO GO TO THE BEACH.
And by going to the beach I don't necessarily mean walking the
boardwalk, playing arcade games, and browsing in the T-shirt
shop. I should say that this is a book for people who like to get
their feet muddy, who are curious about tides and marsh life, who
like to explore little creeks and streams where no one else goes,
people who think that the sound of crashing surf is musical.

I grew up near the beach and have spent much of my adult life
playing around in small boats, hiking beaches, and trying to figure
out how things work in the saltwater environment. There still are
places on the East Coast where you can walk an ocean beach for
miles and not see another person, not see a house or a highway or
a T-shirt shop. These are the places I enjoy and have sought out.
Few of them remain. I call them the last of the coastal wilderness,
and I believe they have the same wilderness values as the canyonlands of Utah or the mountain ranges of Alaska. I lived for two
years in Alaska and found great restorative qualities in hiking and
backpacking in the Kenai Peninsula. I find those same qualities in
walking remote ocean beaches and salt marshes and in canoeing
small creeks where motorboats seldom go. I have nothing against
beach resorts, and frequently enjoy them, but I hope America can
protect the few wild places we have left on our coast. Protecting
these places is like saving an animal from extinction. Once the
wildness is taken from a place, it is taken forever.

This book covers coastal areas in five states, from New Jersey to
North Carolina. If you were to remove the geopolitical bound-
aries—the state lines—the areas would have remarkable similari-
ties. This is the unglaciated coast, a land of sandy beaches, wide
salt marshes, shallow bays, and rivers and creeks that meander

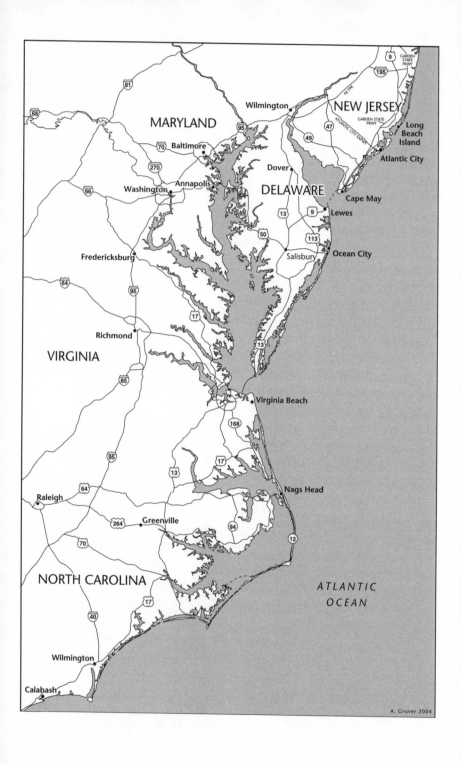

A. Gruver 2004

inland and drain vast regions of upland. Farther north, where glaciers pushed their way down the continent during the last ice age, the coast is more rugged and rocky. We have few rocks on the mid-Atlantic. What we have are sandy barrier islands that sometimes lie miles offshore. The islands act as geological shock absorbers, protecting the mainland from storms and flooding tides. It is one of the world's most productive natural areas, with salt marshes and shallow bays that support a wealth of marine life.

The common denominator in this landscape is grass, specifically cordgrass, *Spartina alterniflora,* which is common between the islands and mainland from New Jersey through North Carolina. These meadows of cordgrass are the building blocks of salt marsh life. They take energy from the sun in photosynthesis, and then release it as the grasses break down in fall and winter, creating a nutrient-rich soup called detritus, which feeds thousands of marine creatures in the shallow bays of the estuary.

The salt marshes and bays have been the economic backbone of many coastal communities for centuries. These waters produce a wealth of clams, crabs, oysters, and fish that are vital to the seafood industry and recreational fishing. This landscape has produced a culture that reflects something of a kinship between coastal people in all five states. In the years following the Civil War, the baymen of the Jersey Shore made a living catching fish and shellfish in the summer and guiding hunting parties in the winter. Watermen in Virginia and North Carolina did the same, building a tradition that is still a vital part of the rural communities along the Atlantic Coast and on the Chesapeake Bay.

North Carolina was especially noted for waterfowl hunting, and for the traditions that came with it. The coast had many hunting clubs, some of which still exist. A few of the grander ones, such as the Whalehead Club in Currituck County, have become museums that capture an earlier life and time along the coast.

Hunters and guides made their own decoys in the late 1800s and early 1900s, and this tradition still lives on through modern artisans. Decoy making and other mediums of wildlife art are celebrated in annual waterfowl festivals all along the coast, in towns such as Tuckerton, Stone Harbor, Medford, Easton, Havre de Grace, Salisbury, Ocean City, Chincoteague, Knotts Island, New Bern, Washington, and Harkers Island. So great is the interest in old decoys that carvings by well-known makers can fetch tens of thousands of dollars.

In writing about wild places it sometimes is easy to concentrate on the birds, animals, and fish one sees and to forget that humans are also a part of the lifescape. In *The Wild Coast* I have sought out places that appeal to me because of their natural attraction, but I have tried to write about the human presence as well. We are, after all, a part of nature, and not above it.

I hope you will enjoy exploring these places as I have, and I hope you will get your feet muddy, listen for music in the surf, find a creek no one has yet explored, and learn a little more about how things work.

The Wild Coast

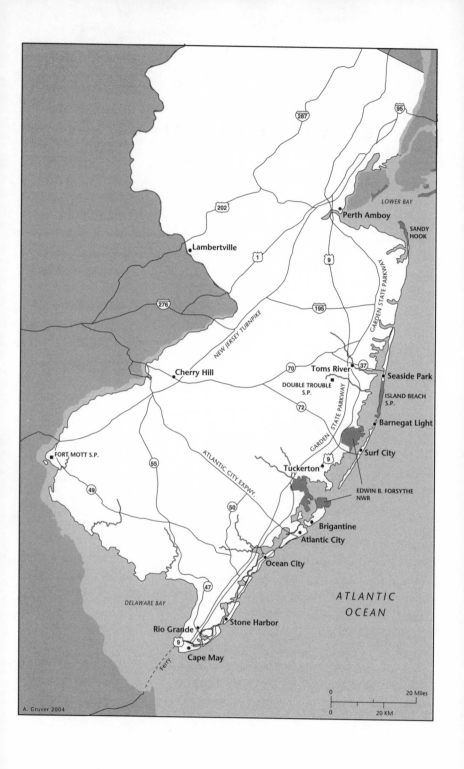

I-287

95

202

LOWER BAY

Perth Amboy

SANDY HOOK

Lambertville

US 1

9

276

GARDEN STATE PARKWAY

NEW JERSEY TURNPIKE

195

70

Cherry Hill

Toms River

37

Seaside Park

DOUBLE TROUBLE
S.P.

ISLAND BEACH
S.P.

72

GARDEN STATE PARKWAY

Barnegat Light

FORT MOTT S.P.

55

ATLANTIC CITY EXPWY.

9

Surf City

Tuckerton

EDWIN B. FORSYTHE
NWR

49

50

Brigantine

Atlantic City

Ocean City

ATLANTIC
OCEAN

47

DELAWARE BAY

Rio Grande

Stone Harbor

9

Ferry

Cape May

0   20 Miles

0   20 KM

A. Gruver 2004

NEW JERSEY

The Gardens of the Garden State

LET'S BE NICE TO NEW JERSEY. HERE WE HAVE THE RODNEY Dangerfield of states, a wonderful parcel of land that separates the Delaware Bay from the Atlantic Ocean and just doesn't get any respect. People read "Garden State" on New Jersey license tags and snicker. New Jersey should be called "the state that glows in the dark," some think. The parts that haven't been paved over are either toxic waste dumps or oil refineries.

None of this is true, of course, although New Jersey is not without blame when it comes to its negative public image. When the New Jersey Turnpike was built, from 1950 to 1952, the state elected to route the 118-mile toll highway through oil refineries, chemical plants, and waste dumps. So for more than a half-century billions of people have driven through New Jersey, many for the first time, and their impression of the state was that it was literally and figuratively a dump.

A much more fitting introduction to New Jersey would be the Garden State Parkway, which begins in Cape May and winds its way northward along the coast to Perth Amboy. Driving north, you can look to your right and see miles of salt marsh, meandering creeks, and tidal bays, with the barrier beaches far in the distance. On your left will be the New Jersey Pine Barrens, hundreds of square miles of pitch pine forest that the state has wisely protected. The pine barrens are the major source of groundwater for cities such as Philadelphia and Camden, and they remain today as wild and remote as when John McPhee made them famous in his 1968 book *The Pine Barrens* (New York: Farrar, Straus & Giroux).

The Garden State Parkway is a toll highway built for speed, but it passes through places that invite the driver to slow down, get off the parkway, and explore. For example, just north of Cape May, near Stone Harbor, the Wetlands Institute overlooks a sweeping salt marsh. There is a hiking trail, a museum and aquarium, and a tower that offers a view for miles along the salt marsh and barrier island chain. The mission of the Wetlands Institute is to promote an appreciation for coastal ecosystems, and its education programs are designed with this as a priority. Guided tours are available, and various public programs are held throughout the year.

Farther along, you can stop at the Brigantine and Barnegat divisions of the Edwin B. Forsythe National Wildlife Refuge. Little Egg Harbor is interesting to explore, and if you're in no great hurry, you can take state Route 9 up to Barnegat from Tuckerton to get a feel for the Jersey coast as it was a century or more ago. Tuckerton Seaport is a restored maritime village that provides a great introduction to the human and natural histories of the Little Egg Harbor and Long Beach areas. Waterfowl hunting, fishing, and shellfish harvesting were the backbone of the economy here in the 1800s, and the seaport gives visitors a glimpse of what life as a bayman was like.

Farther north, you can exit the parkway at milepost 77 and within minutes be in the pine barrens. Double Trouble State Park is near the town of Toms River, and it has trails, a restored village, and an old cranberry bog. The park is the site of a former lumber mill and cranberry business. The Double Trouble Company was incorporated in 1909 by Edward Crabbe and George Bunker. They operated a sawmill here, and between 1910 and 1926 they planted more than two hundred acres of cranberry vines. The bog became the largest in the state, and Double Trouble became one of New Jersey's largest cranberry producers. The historic village includes the mill, the cranberry packing building, a school, housing for workers, among other buildings. There are miles of trails and sand roads running through the pine forest—a good place to see birds, especially during the spring and fall migrations.

New Jersey Route 9 and the Garden State Parkway are part of the state's Coastal Heritage Trail, which was established in 1988 to foster public appreciation of the state's vast coastal resources along the Atlantic Ocean and the Delaware bayshore. In recent years the state has done an excellent job of promoting awareness of the natural history and human history of the coast, and of protecting and restoring coastal resources. The trail begins on the west at Fort Mott State Park on the Delaware Bay near Deepwater and runs southward to Cape May and then northward up the Atlantic Coast to the Sandy Hook area.

Few of the barrier beaches of the New Jersey shore are undeveloped, but there still are places where a visitor can walk a few miles of wild beach or hike dune trails through a maritime forest. Island Beach State Park near Toms River has more than eight miles of undeveloped shoreline, and the Sandy Hook area, in the densely populated northern part of the state, is included in the Gateway National Recreation Area, which includes Breezy Point, Jamaica Bay, Staten Island, and other sites in New York.

Unlike most of the New Jersey shore, Sandy Hook is virtually undeveloped and boasts some of the most remarkable natural features on the mid–Atlantic Coast. An old-growth holly forest has trees more than 150 years old. Stand on the North Beach of Sandy Hook, and if the skies are reasonably clear, you will see Breezy Point across the waters of Rockaway Inlet.

Sandy Hook is the southern gateway of the New York harbor, and over the years it has served the New York environs in a number of ways. The original Sandy Hook Lighthouse was built in 1764, and it, or its replacements, has guided ships into the harbor ever since. Sandy Hook has played a role in national defense at least since the War of 1812, when the army first built permanent fortifications. Fort Hancock and a series of gun batteries were built in the late 1800s, and they served until 1974, when the fort was decommissioned and transferred to Gateway NRA. Today, many of the buildings of Fort Hancock are used by environmental groups and researchers studying the flora and fauna of this coastal ecosystem. The U.S. Coast Guard operates its Sandy Hook station on the northern tip of the peninsula, and it is the only remaining military presence.

The 6.5-mile-long peninsula does get its share of human visitors, especially during the summer, but management practices

protect the rich natural habitats of Sandy Hook. In June and July
you'll find crowds of people swimming and working on their tans,
but adjacent to them, across a well-marked barrier, there will be
endangered piping plovers, least and common terns, black skimmers, and oystercatchers. In recent years, some thirty-five pairs of
plovers have been nesting on the beach, making it one of the most
productive plover colonies per acre on the coast. Special wire
enclosures built by park personnel protect the nesting birds by
eliminating large predators such as raccoons, gulls, and feral cats.

The most important natural asset of Sandy Hook is the holly
forest along Spermaceti Cove just west of the ranger station. A trail
begins at a boardwalk overlook on the south side of the forest, and
then winds through a high marsh, a shrub thicket, and finally
through the grove of hollies. Some of the trees are 150 years old or
more, and while their trunks are massive, the upper limbs have
been pruned and twisted by the many storms that have buffeted
this barrier island environment. The holly is a hardy plant, however, and it has adapted well to the sandy soil, salt air, and occasional northeaster.

Perhaps the greatest danger to the holly forest came around the
turn of the century when visitors would come to Sandy Hook to
cut holly for Christmas decorations. As the number of holly cut-
ters increased—and perhaps as a market for holly became established on the mainland—the trees became endangered. The army
at Fort Hancock came to the rescue, posting guards at the holly
forest prior to the holiday season.

The holly forest is a unique and valuable natural resource for
several reasons. It is the only such stand remaining in the region,
and the trees are popular with birds, which nest among the thick,
spiked leaves and feed on the red berries. The hollies also have a
thick understory of greenbrier, poison ivy, Virginia creeper, and
honeysuckle, and this thicket is home to a wide variety of birds
and animals. It may not be a garden in the formal, conventional
sense, but here on the New Jersey coast, it's one of the brighter
blossoms of the Garden State.

Cape May

A day at the beach is filled with surprises

On my first trip to Higbee Beach, several years ago, I was looking for birds on a dune trail that wound its way through a shrub thicket and led to a sandy beach on Delaware Bay. I was carrying a camera, binoculars, and a notepad, and I had my lunch and extra film in a daypack. I was wearing shorts, a T-shirt, and hiking boots.

I walked across the dune, emerged from the thicket, and found myself among a group of about thirty people who were wearing nothing but a smile and a suntan. A man of about sixty approached me. He was the color of mahogany and had skin that needed saddle soap. To his credit, he didn't seem at all shocked to see a fully clothed person there on the beach. At Higbee Beach they're used to having bird-watchers around.

"See anything interesting?" he asked, gesturing toward the binoculars.

"Yellow-rumps," I answered. "The dunes are full of them."

He looked at me quizzically. "Warblers," I added. "Yellow-rumped warblers. They're migrating through by the thousands right now."

Lynn and I went back to Higbee Beach more recently and found that the yellow-rumps were still there. The mahogany man and his friends were not. Lynn hadn't been with me on the first trip, and I think she was disappointed.

Higbee Beach is in Cape May, on the very southern tip of New Jersey, and when bird-watchers come here it's like baseball fans going to Cooperstown. Cape May is a beautiful seaside resort with Victorian homes, interesting shops, and an ocean-side promenade, but people come here for the birds. In fall and winter it's for the migrating hawks and waterfowl. In spring it's to witness the

thousands of migrating shorebirds that flock to the beaches to
feed on the eggs of horseshoe crabs.

Cape May, like Virginia's Eastern Shore, is a migratory funnel.
Coastal New Jersey is flanked by the Atlantic on one side and
Delaware Bay on the other. At the cape, the peninsula narrows to
only a few miles in width. Here, birds gather in impressive num-
bers before heading across Delaware Bay and on to Delaware,
Maryland, Virginia, and points south.

Bird-watchers also gather in impressive numbers in the Cape
May region, providing a significant economic boost to this beach
town, with a pre- and post-summer influx of binocular-toting,
cash-spending visitors. New Jersey has been quick to recognize
the value of this birding
phenomenon and has
created the Coastal
Heritage Trail, a
visitor-oriented
compendium of
refuges, parks, pre-
serves, and historical
sites along the Delaware
bayshore and the Atlantic
Coast. While Cape May has
been known among birders for

Yellow-rumped warbler

decades, the intent of the Coastal Heritage Trail is to encourage
visitors to explore other areas along the bay and the coast.

The Cape May area, the southern tip of the peninsula, is still the
magnet that draws birds and those who watch them, and much of
this area has been protected either by state, federal, or private conservation groups. Just south of town, on the Atlantic, is the Nature
Conservancy's Cape May Migratory Bird Refuge. South of that is
Cape May Point State Park, where the lighthouse and hawk observation platform are located. Higbee Beach, a state wildlife management area, is just around the tip, and it comprises the last
forested dune system on the bayshore. Nearby is Hidden Valley,
another conservancy preserve consisting mainly of forest, grass-

land, and shrub thickets. Farther north on the bay is Cape May National Wildlife Refuge and several other conservancy preserves, wildlife management areas, and state forests.

The dozen or so square miles that make up the tip of the Cape May peninsula are a naturalist's delight. Whether your interest is birds, butterflies, native plants, beach dynamics, or whale watching, there is something here for you—and at virtually any time of year.

The reason, of course, is habitat, and Cape May has a wonderfully diverse range of natural environments packed into an area you could comfortably tour by bicycle in a single day. The Cape May area includes the ocean beach of Cape May proper, residential West Cape May, and Cape May Point, where the Delaware Bay estuary meets the ocean currents of the Atlantic. The land here is essentially an island, removed from mainland New Jersey by the Cape May Canal portion of the Intracoastal Waterway and by Cape May Harbor to the east. Access is by the Garden State Parkway, which becomes Lafayette Street when it enters town, and by Seashore Road, also known as state Route 626.

This tiny island, this quiet resort with its Victorian charm, offers an amazing variety for naturalists of all interests and abilities. There is ocean beach, bay beach, dunes, tidal flats, brackish streams and ponds, salt marshes, hardwood swamps, meadows, pine and deciduous forests, and carefully cultivated butterfly gardens. While the beach attracts its summer tourists, and Cape May supports a substantial population of year-round residents, there is a remarkable amount of undeveloped land here, thanks to the efforts of federal, state, and local agencies, as well as private conservation groups such as the New Jersey Audubon Society and the Nature Conservancy. Those responsible for planning the future of Cape May have wisely factored the natural assets of the area into the equation, and they have proved that preservation of the coastal ecosystem can pay economic dividends to the region and improve the quality of life. Cape May and southern New Jersey draw tens of thousands of visitors each year who come for the birds, the butterflies, and the whales. Perhaps these assets lack the glitter of casinos and nightclubs, but the economics of nature-oriented tourism are real.

So Cape May offers a day at the beach, fine dining, graceful accommodations, friendly people, and some of the best nature watching you'll come across on this planet. What follows is a close-up look at some specific sites in the Cape May area—south of the Cape May Canal—that offer public access and some extraordinary natural history experiences.

CAPE MAY MIGRATORY BIRD REFUGE

Perhaps the logical place to begin a naturalist's tour of Cape May would be on Sunset Boulevard, state Route 606, where it intersects with Route 626, one of the main access roads linking the cape with the rest of the world. If you're coming from the beach, turn left (west) onto Sunset between the small shopping center and convenience store. The first stopping point would be the Cape May Migratory Bird Refuge, about one mile down on the left.

This preserve is owned by the Nature Conservancy and includes 187 acres of beach, brackish marshland, and spring-fed freshwater ponds and adjacent meadowlands. It is on the site of South Cape May, a Victorian resort community incorporated in 1884 that was destroyed by storms in the early 1950s. The foundations of many of the stately buildings of what was South Cape May now lie beyond the surf line. Others have long since been removed, and in more recent years the land that makes up the preserve has been used for farming, cattle grazing, and even as a private airstrip. Where the parking lot is now located once stood the southernmost store in New Jersey, a custard stand appropriately named Custard's Last Stand.

The conservancy bought the site in 1981 and has been managing it as a migratory bird refuge. Endangered piping plovers and least terns nest in the shell litter on the wide beach, and sandpipers, sanderlings, and a host of other beach birds forage in the wet sand behind retreating breakers. Leeward of the dunes are shallow ponds, brackish and freshwater marshland, and meadows.

Public access to the preserve is via a one-mile hiking loop that begins and ends in the parking lot on Sunset Boulevard. The trail heads south across meadow and marsh along what once was Sixteenth Street in South Cape May, offering excellent views of the fields and ponds from an elevated platform. The path crosses the dune line and extends along the beach for less than a quarter of a mile, then heads back north along another section of meadow, ending in the parking area.

It's a fairly short walk, but it should be done at a leisurely pace; there's a lot to see in these 187 acres. As its name suggests, the preserve's main clientele are migratory birds. This would mean, most notably, the piping plovers and least terns that nest each spring on the beach. With so much of the Atlantic coastline having been developed over the past century, the expanses of wild beach favored by these birds are at a premium. The conservancy has protected a significant chunk of it here, and it is prime plover habitat: high, wide beach just beyond the longest lick of high tide, covered with shell litter that serves as camouflage for eggs and nestlings.

Each spring the nesting sites are roped off and enclosures are erected to protect nesting birds from predators such as gulls, fish crows, and a variety of mammals, including house cats and domestic dogs. Still, the plovers and terns face a tough battle for survival. Spring storms can cause high tides that inundate nests, and if the storms occur late enough in the season, the birds may not renest. The list of predators is long, including other birds, mammals, and even ghost crabs, which are plentiful within the plover-tern colony.

Least terns and piping plovers can be seen at the preserve from early spring throughout the summer. But if you go, stay behind the roped-off area and keep your distance from birds that may be nesting or feeding outside the boundary.

The beach and the viewing platforms are excellent venues for the fall hawk migration, which begins in late August and extends into November. Like most bird migrations, the passage of hawks during the fall is driven by the weather, a cold front often bringing with it hundreds of birds. The Cape May peninsula is famous for its fall hawk migration, and this preserve is one of the favored viewing locations, along with neighboring Cape May State Park.

The brackish marsh is a good place to see a variety of plants, which include some that prefer a saltwater environment such as the *Spartinas,* and others like grasses and reeds that are more often associated with a less saline environment. After years of use as a cattle pasture, the meadow is reverting to woody growth, with cedars, marsh elder, and various other shrub species.

Migrating butterflies and dragonflies use the meadow as a resting area, and it's one of the best spots in Cape May to see monarch butterflies when they come through on their way to wintering grounds in Central America.

The ponds are home to numerous waterfowl species during migration, and there are nesting pairs of dabbling ducks such as blue-winged teal, gadwall, and black duck. Terns, herons, egrets, willets, and glossy ibises are common visitors, and red-winged blackbirds nest in the stands of cattails and phragmites, which also provide temporary shelter for migrating bobolinks. Mammals include deer, gray and red fox, skunk, mink, weasel, raccoon, and opossum.

The trail is an easy hike, and the entrance and observation platform are wheelchair accessible.

CAPE MAY POINT STATE PARK

Next door to the Nature Conservancy's Cape May Migratory Bird Refuge is Cape May State Park, which among birders is internationally famous for its fall hawk watch. The hawk watch platform is across the parking lot from the lighthouse and visitor center and overlooks the ocean, a World War II–era bunker that now is in the surf zone, and the ponds and marshes of the state park and conservancy property.

Cape May's reputation as a birding hotspot is based in large part upon the great number of hawks counted each fall from the platform. Also contributing to the image is the spring shorebird phenomenon, when horseshoe crabs clamber ashore by the millions and lay eggs, in turn attracting hordes of migrating shorebirds, which feast on the eggs as they replenish fat reserves during their trip northward to breeding grounds in the Arctic.

The hawk platform, run by the New Jersey Audubon Society, is most active from late August into November, when people come from all over the world to watch hawks. The hawk migration, like most bird movement, is weather driven. A cold front, with a stiff northeast breeze, will push through great waves of raptors (birds of prey).

Cooper's hawk

New Jersey Audubon employs an official hawk counter for the fall migration, but the official counter is usually accompanied by dozens of other birders of a wide variety of experience. Some come for only an hour or so; others spend days. A great account of the experiences, personalities, and indeed the politics of watching and banding hawks is Jack Connor's book *Season at the Point: The Birds and Birders of Cape May* (New York: Atlantic Monthly Press, 1991).

While the hawk platform is busiest in the fall, it also provides an excellent venue for watching seabirds during the dead of winter. All three North American scoters can be seen, as well as oldsquaw, eiders, and occasionally pelagic species such as northern gannets.

A butterfly garden attracts both butterflies and the lepidopterists who come to see them. Cape May County has 104 species of butterflies, with the area at the point a good place to spot the occasional vagrant from the south. The marsh meadows are a good place to look for Aaron's Skipper, which was discovered in Cape May in 1890 by Dr. Henry Skinner of Philadelphia. This salt marsh skipper is still found in Cape May County, one of the few places in New Jersey it still frequents.

New Jersey Audubon's Cape May Bird Observatory, across the street from the state park, also has a butterfly garden, as well as a wealth of information on the natural history of the Cape May region. The organization regularly sponsors group trips highlighting birds, butterflies, plants, wildflowers, whale watching, and other subjects of seasonal interest.

HIGBEE BEACH WILDLIFE MANAGEMENT AREA AND HIDDEN VALLEY

Mention Cape May to a birding enthusiast in, let's say, Minnesota, and you'll get two responses: the great fall hawk migration and the spring horseshoe crab/shorebird phenomenon. Among birders, spring at Cape May evokes images of a great seafood omelet—billions and billions of horseshoe crab eggs being scavenged by tens of thousands of shorebirds, all refueling for the last legs of their trip north. We've all read the articles, seen the photos of horseshoe crabs stacked atop each other like discarded World War I army helmets, and seen the Discovery Channel videos of shorebirds flying in unison like a school of fish.

True. All true. But visit the woods, the upland meadows, and the hardwood swamps of Higbee, and you'll discover another facet of birding at Cape May that the nature news media often overlook. The cape, like most peninsulas in a major flyway, acts as a migratory funnel, channeling birds down a narrow chute, stacking them up in avian traffic jams when the weather is just so. In the spring and fall Cape May is temporary home to countless neotropical migrant birds—the warblers, tanagers, thrushes, and other species that spend their winters in the tropics and then travel to the northern United States and Canada in the spring to raise their young.

The great warbler traffic at Cape May is sometimes overlooked, perhaps because the warblers are less accessible, more difficult to see and identify, and lack the sex appeal of migrating hawks or shorebirds having a crab-omelet-to-go as they head for the Arctic. After all, a peregrine falcon stooping on a resident rock dove at the World War II bunker at the state park gets the adrenaline flowing; it brings out the machismo in bird-watching, it's an in-your-face slam-dunk.

The woods of Higbee are filled with mystery. In early summer the leaves are minty green, fresh. A figure moves among them far overhead. It darts from limb to limb . . . too quick to raise the binoculars. Suddenly it appears in an island of sunlight, and you see a bird whose breast is impossibly yellow, so bright and colorful it seems unreal, especially in this dark woods full of cool greens and earthy browns.

You scramble through the warbler section of the field guide, finding all sorts of birds with yellow breasts. And then like an apparition the little bird alights just above you, and you see for the first time the black flecks on the sides, the rusty patch on the back, the yellow eyebrow. You learn that it's a prairie warbler, and as you're watching it through the binoculars it sings its rising little trill, and you realize in a second not only what kind of bird it is but what its song is like.

Such little victories, it seems to me, are worth a lot—perhaps more than watching red knots stand wing-to-wing on a beach, perhaps even more than seeing a peregrine reduce a pigeon to a puff of feathers drifting on the wind.

In Cape May, Higbee and Hidden Valley are the places to have these experiences, these close encounters with warblers and their kin. Higbee and Hidden Valley are just north of Cape May State Park and are accessed by state Route 641, New England Road. Higbee Beach Wildlife Management Area (WMA) is a six-hundred-acre tract owned and managed by the New Jersey Division of Fish, Game, and Wildlife. Hidden Valley Ranch is a two-hundred-acre parcel recently added to the WMA. Parking for Hidden Valley is in a small lot on the left on Route 641. A trail begins at the parking lot, cuts across a grassy meadow, and enters a forested section and hardwood swamp. The meadow area is a prime spot for butterflies and wildflowers, while the wooded area is great for birding.

The best times to see migratory songbirds are the few weeks during spring and fall when the birds are moving between their nesting sites in North America and wintering grounds in the tropics. This would mean mid-April to late May and late August to November for most species. The early portion of the fall migration seems to produce the greatest variety of birds, with a few surprises always possible. Yellow-rumped warblers dominate the later periods of the migration.

Birding is good at Hidden Valley year round, with many resident species on hand. Prothonotary warblers and scarlet tanagers nest in the wooded areas, and orchard orioles, white-eyed vireos, indigo buntings, and blue grosbeaks nest in the meadows and shrub communities.

Higbee Beach WMA is just down the road from Hidden Valley and includes hiking trails, beach access, and a butterfly garden. Until the late 1990s, Higbee had the distinction of being well known among those who enjoy getting a suntan without the bother of tan lines. Unfortunately, Higbee also gained a somewhat notorious reputation for naughty behavior, and state and city officials intervened, eliminating what unofficially was a "clothing optional" section of beach. Higbee has since become a popular family beach and is part of the hiking trails that wind through the WMA. The beach is wide and clean, and marked trails make the dune thickets and maritime forest easily accessible. Those paths are good venues for seeing migrating songbirds in spring and fall.

BENNETT BOGS PRESERVE

For admirers of wildflowers and native plants, this twenty-five-acre preserve in Cape May is a real gem. It offers some of the rarest plants in New Jersey, abundant wildlife, and even has a place in the history of the resort community.

Bennett Bogs Preserve is located on Shunpike Road, just off Route 647. More than 250 species of plants have been identified here, including maiden-cane grass, wrinkled jointgrass, Torrey's dropseed, and the Pine Barren gentian, which blooms in the fall.

The term "bogs" is something of a misnomer when applied to these wetlands. They more accurately are vernal ponds, which flood in winter and spring and dry out in summer and fall. It is during the dry stages that the great display of wildflowers, sedges, and rushes appears. Until fairly recent years these wetlands were considered wastelands and were treated accordingly. Many vernal ponds along the mid–Atlantic Coast have been filled and developed, so the three at Bennett Bogs provide a look at a special natural system that remains much as it was when the Native Americans hunted here.

The ponds have seen their share of human activity, however. When the resort community of Cape May was built in the late 1800s, clay was taken from the ponds to make bricks for the hotels. Farmers once harvested hay and wild cranberries from the wet meadows, and children skated on the ponds in winter.

The natural values of the ponds were first noticed by botanists Bayard Long and S. S. Van Pelt, whose 1907 report on rare plants at Bennett Bogs drew the attention of the scientific community. The New Jersey Audubon Society purchased six acres at the site and created the Bennett Bogs Preserve in 1955. The Nature Conservancy joined the effort in 1984, adding another nineteen acres and thus establishing a forested buffer around the three ponds. The preserve is jointly managed by both conservation organizations.

The best time to visit the preserve is late summer and early fall, when the wetland plants are usually in bloom. Butterflies, dragonflies, and damselflies also frequent the area, as do migrating songbirds and resident birds, including waders such as green herons. The shallow ponds and the trails that run along them will be wet until mid- to late summer, depending upon the amount of rainfall.

Along the Bayshore

Exploring New Jersey's wild side

I left Cape May one warm spring morning, picked up state Route 47 at Rio Grande, and headed north, looking for horseshoe crabs. It didn't take me long to find them. If you turn left off Route 47, you soon will find yourself looking at Delaware Bay. And if you time it right, the beaches will be filled with horseshoe crabs and with the birds that come to feast on crab eggs.

The conventional wisdom is that the crabs come ashore during the full moon in late May to lay their eggs. The large females, having been fertilized by males in the shallow water near shore, slowly make their way out of the water and lay huge masses of eggs on the sandy beach. Few of the eggs survive to become adult horseshoe crabs; most are eaten by migrating shorebirds, which stop on Delaware Bay beaches to refuel on their way to nesting grounds in the Arctic.

On my trip to the New Jersey bayshore I missed the shorebirds by just a few days. It was early June, the full moon had passed, and so had the red knots and sandpipers, which by now were probably somewhere over Canada, burning fat reserves they had acquired on these narrow beaches a short while ago. But there still were horseshoe crabs, and instead of shorebirds there were great flocks of gulls feeding on the eggs that remained.

Driving along the Delaware Bay in New Jersey is a great pleasure, no matter what the season. This is a part of New Jersey that visitors seldom see. It is a rural area with a decidedly southern feel. There are small towns and farm fields, salt marshes and vast tracts of pine forest. Small mom-and-pop restaurants sell homemade chicken salad and cole slaw. There are old waterfront towns, little beach communities, and roadside markets selling tomatoes and lima beans.

While the Atlantic Coast of New Jersey is intensely developed, the bayshore remains emphatically rural. There are no hotel chains, luxury condominiums, or amusement parks. The towns are small, the people are friendly, and the hospitality is genuine. What we have here is Mayberry above the Mason-Dixon line.

I drove north, taking every left turn I could find, and discovered an eclectic collection of bayshore beach communities. Just north of the Cape May ferry terminal is Beach Road. This two-lane street runs northward from the ferry terminal along the beachfront. Several public access points are along the road, and at some places the beach can be seen from the road itself, a good place to look for birds during the spring migration. The area is residential, though, and most of the property is privately owned.

I followed the signs from Beach Road to Route 603, which intersects with Route 47, and drove to Reed's Beach, which is at the end of Route 655, a short distance off Route 47. There is a small marina here, with two viewing platforms—one on the beach and the other in the marina parking lot. A modest fee is charged.

Hand's Landing, named for Absolom Hand, one of the early European settlers in Cape May County, is part of a large protected area owned by the Nature Conservancy and Cape May National Wildlife Refuge (NWR). It includes beachfront, salt marsh, freshwater wetlands, and forested upland. Hand's Landing is a relatively new preserve purchased by the conservancy in 1997. It includes 112 acres and more than 1,000 feet of sandy beach. A viewing area is at the end of Hand's Landing Road, off Route 47. Hand's Landing is adjacent to Kimble's Beach and Cape May NWR, whose headquarters are on Hand's Landing Road.

I took Glade Road from Route 47, turned onto East Point Road, and followed it to the end. The beach is a short distance from the parking area. This is part of Heislerville Wildlife Management Area, at the mouth of the Maurice River. Thompson's Beach is just east of here, and Fortescue and Gandy's Beach are a little farther north. The Nature Conservancy owns and manages a seven-hundred-acre preserve at Gandy's Beach, which includes nearly a half mile of good beachfront shorebird habitat. A viewing kiosk and a nature trail are located along the beach.

As I drove along the bayshore I was pleased to find that much of the waterfront is protected either through state, federal, or private conservation ownership. The Cape May Audubon head-quarters are on Route 47, as is the Nature Conservancy's Delaware bayshore office. Cape May National Wildlife Refuge is one of the newest in our national system, and it is growing fast, with the goal of protecting more than sixteen thousand acres on the Cape May peninsula. There are numerous state wildlife management areas, state forests, and preserves owned by the Nature Conservancy.

So when it comes to this narrow peninsula of southern New Jersey, with Cape May at its tip, the Delaware bayshore is definitely New Jersey's wild side.

Island Beach

The past is preserved on the Jersey Shore

On July 1, 1953, at the New Jersey State Museum in Trenton, Governor Alfred E. Driscoll accepted the title to a nine-mile-long ribbon of sand called Island Beach, a barrier spit about a half mile wide that separates Barnegat Bay from the Atlantic Ocean. It was a golden moment for conservationists, who had long fought to protect what essentially was the last intact barrier island ecosystem in the state. Driscoll signed the deed, handed over a check for $2.7 million to the former owners, and in a matter of minutes, history had been written.

The first time I went to Island Beach I hiked a trail that wound through a thicket of pitch pine and cedar, then crossed a heather bald and climbed to the crest of the primary dune. Miles of open beach stretched before me, and the ocean flexed slowly and broke lazily onto the beach. To the south lay Barnegat Inlet, and on the far shore was Barnegat Lighthouse. Behind me were miles of maritime forest and salt marsh, cedars and pines pruned and stunted by salt wind, and little salt ponds and tidal guts that meandered through marsh meadows.

Years earlier I had met the naturalist and writer John Terres, whom I had interviewed for a magazine story and who became a good friend. When we first met, John mentioned Island Beach and spoke with pride of his role in protecting it. At the time the park was created, he was the editor of *Audubon* magazine, and that organization played a leading role in the protection of the island. Later, he wrote in his book *The Wonders I See* (Philadelphia: Lippincott, 1960) of climbing to the crest of a primary dune and seeing for the first time the open ocean, the beach that melted uninterrupted into the horizon, and the broad bay that separated the island from the mainland. In seeing the same panorama for the first time, I immediately understood John's passion for protecting the place. He described a trip in the fall of 1950 this way: "As I reached a dune's top, the whole panorama of ocean and sky suddenly lay before me—an immense vault of blue above, the limitless gray ocean below, stretching away to the eastern horizon to meet the fire of the rising sun. Often the great beauty and loneliness of scenes like this are almost overpowering, yet here, for the first time in my life, I felt as though I stood alone on the morning of Creation."

Island Beach is near the town of Toms River, which is on the river of the same name, which empties into Barnegat Bay. Take state Route 37 east and you will soon be on the island, which technically became a peninsula after a storm in 1812 closed Cranberry Inlet, near the community of Seaside Heights. Upon reaching the island, you can turn left (north) and reach the more populated sections of the Jersey Shore, or you can turn right and find yourself in Island Beach in about five minutes.

The state park is just outside the communities of Seaside Heights and Seaside Park, which pretty much mingle on either side of state Route 35, the main roadway that runs along the spine of the island. These communities are what many people think of when they hear mention of the Jersey Shore. A wooden boardwalk and an amusement park are pure Americana. There are games of chance and vendors selling cheesesteak subs and sausage sandwiches. The aroma is a promising combination of suntan oil, fried onions, and salt breeze. The motels are small, family-operated businesses, with names like Charlroy, Bay Breeze, Sea Gull, Flamingo, Palm Villa, Sea Gem, Sea Breeze, and Sea View. There is not a Hilton or a Hyatt in sight.

I spent a few days in Seaside Park, staying in a small motel that advertised air conditioning and color television. I had a second-floor corner room with the room number drawn on the door with a Magic Marker. The motel was of the vintage when air conditioners were built into the wall under the window. The second-floor

rooms were reached by taking a wooden stairway, which was outside the building. The view, through a small window caked with
salt, was of a parking lot, the street, the boardwalk, and the beach.

Seaside Park is a thoroughly captivating community, with a little restaurant just down the street run by an Italian couple and
their son, who opened at seven and served nothing but breakfast
until 3 P.M., at which time they closed for the day. I spent hours
walking the boardwalk and peering into the clapboard shops
where young people played video games. I ate cheesesteaks and
took pictures of the wonderfully garish paintings that decorated
the amusement park. I sat on boardwalk benches with men wearing Bermuda shorts and black socks, watching teenage girls walk
by with towels wrapped around their waists, their hair sleek and
matted down by seawater.

The Barnegat Lighthouse

And it occurred to me that this was the kind of thing my friend
John Terres, the Audubon Society, and all of the conservationists
back in 1950 were trying to prevent happening at Island Beach.
And it further occurred to me that now, more than fifty years later,
it is this community, and perhaps hundreds more like it, that is
endangered. The truth is, beachfront property is too valuable for
motels that have air conditioners in the windows. It is too exclusive for restaurants that sell $4.50 cheesesteaks, for shops that sell
dollar chances on teddy bears.

A few weeks earlier, I had been on the Outer Banks of North
Carolina. The northern beaches, near the town of Corolla, had
been covered with luxury condos, shopping centers, expensive
hotels, and fine restaurants. While walking the boardwalk in Seaside Park, I couldn't help but believe that someday soon the same
would happen here, that the small family motels and restaurants
were living on borrowed time and would one day be flattened and
removed and replaced with buildings much finer and more expensive. And it seemed very sad, the prospect of losing this little seam
of American culture, an authentic and intact icon from the 1950s.

Island Beach State Park is an island in more ways than one. The
New Jersey shore is intensely developed from Cape May to Sandy
Hook, but here you drive through the entry gate and experience a
barrier beach as it might have been when the Europeans arrived in
the seventeenth century. It is an island of wild beach in a sea of
boardwalks and cheesesteak stands. It is not a wilderness beach
like those of the Virginia coast, but it is as close to the real thing as
we're likely to find in New Jersey.

Island Beach has a wide constituency. I parked in the southern-
most lot in the park, and a woman in the car next to mine was
dressed in patriotic bike tights. She wore shorts with blue and
white stripes, a top that was red with white stars, and from the
trunk of her car she pulled a red racing bike. Soon she was off
down the bike lane that parallels the two-lane road that runs the
length of the park, the star-spangled bicyclist heading north to
Seaside Park.

Later, in the parking lot of the park office, I watched a man driving an old blue Chevy station wagon. He had with him a huge, shaggy white dog, which the driver kept on a leash that he held through the window as he slowly drove around the perimeter of the parking lot. When he stopped the car, the dog would bark incessantly until he would drive again, and then the dog would trot happily alongside the car.

The parking lots had buses filled with day-tripping school kids, cars from a wide variety of states, beach buggies driven by surf fishermen, SUVs with bike racks, and trailers with canoes. There were even a few of us wandering around with binoculars and bird guides, peering into the thickets for the golden flash of a warbler.

The wild and the not-so-wild have coexisted here for close to a half century, since Island Beach State Park opened to the public on Memorial Day weekend in 1959. If you want to see the wild side of Island Beach, the first thing to do is to park the car, get away from the parking lots and the people, and hit the trails. The park is divided into recreational zones and natural areas, and the latter are the places to see the island in its unaltered state. The northern natural area begins just inside the park boundary and extends for about three miles. The southern natural area covers about three miles on the southern tip of the island. The three miles in the middle are designated recreational zone, which is where you'll find the bathhouse, comfort station, beach access for sport fishing, and men walking their dogs from old Chevy wagons.

I drove down Central Avenue from Seaside Park, passed the last of the retail establishments, paid four dollars to the uniformed gatekeeper, and soon was looking at the Jersey Shore as Henry Hudson might have found it. Well . . . minus the road, the office, the bathhouse, and the tollgate.

Aeolium Nature Center Trail is on the left, just behind the small nature center. I parked the car and walked it. It's a short trail, about a quarter-mile loop, but it gives the visitor a great introduction to the landscape of Island Beach. The trail winds through dune thickets and heather balds and runs along the primary dune for a short distance before returning to the nature center. It's a short walk, but you can see red and white cedars, pitch pine, southern red oak, American holly, and shadbush, or serviceberry, which flowers in late March and early April, just as the shad head upriver to spawn. The flowers of the shadbush become purple berries by midsummer and are a favorite of the bird population. Beach plum is also common in the dune thickets. It flowers in mid-May, and the wild plums ripen in late summer, providing food for birds and small mammals such as red foxes. Local people gather the plums to make jelly.

A feature of Island Beach not found on southern coasts are the heather balds. Just off Aeolium Trail the entire face of a dune is covered with heather (*Hudsonia tomentosa*), along with a variety of lichens. Heather is a "sand catcher," and it protects the dunes from wind and rain. The thick, low-growing plants trap moving sand, and the roots and stems help stabilize the dunes. Naturalists say that some of the heather balds on Island Beach are more than seventy-five years old.

The secondary dunes and the thickets are the best places to see wildlife. On Aeolium Trail, gray catbirds were scampering through the thickets, and now and then I caught a glimpse of a common yellowthroat. The trail gives a good introduction to both the dune and thicket plant communities. Some of the common plants of the secondary dunes are dusty miller, poison ivy, goldenrod, cactus, bayberry, and beach pea, all of which provide a food source for wild birds and mammals.

The thickets have sumac, beach plum, wild black cherry, green-brier, red cedar, and dewberry, and the forests are mainly made up of American holly, white cedar, pin oak, white oak, willow oak, and pitch pine, which is the predominant plant of the New Jersey Pine Barrens, which lie just a few miles inland of Island Beach.

For a slender and fragile piece of land, Island Beach has a great diversity of plant habitat. I hiked the primary and secondary dunes, the shrub thickets, and a maritime forest, and then crossed the island to discover Barnegat Bay. The park has five trails that lead from parking areas through woodland, freshwater wetlands, salt marsh, and finally to the shallow waters of the bay. One of my favorites is Spizzle Trail near the southern end of the park, between parking lots nineteen and twenty. This is a round-trip walk of about a mile that begins in a cedar thicket just off the main road. The trail leads to a bird blind on the shore of Barnegat Bay that is a great place to watch waterfowl in the fall and winter. In other seasons you're likely to see egrets, oystercatchers, willets, and various gulls. A nesting platform for ospreys is a short distance from the blind. The thickets and wetlands along the trail are good places to look for songbirds, especially during the spring and fall migrations. While at parking lot nineteen, take advantage of the expansive view from atop the primary dune.

Perhaps the best birding trail on Island Beach is Johnny Allen's Cove Trail near the interpretive center. This trail offers two options. One branch crosses the dunes and leads to the ocean, and another crosses wetlands and salt marsh and ends on the shore of Barnegat Bay. The ocean trail winds through a wooded area and dense thicket, a good place to look for songbirds. The bay trail offers some of the best birding in the park, because it crosses a diverse range of habitats in a short distance. There is freshwater wetland, salt marsh, shrub thickets, and forest. The trail leads along the edge of the wetlands and salt marsh, and this edge habitat is the place to look for birds. May and October are the best times to see migrating warblers and other songbirds.

The salt marshes and shallow bay are filled with waterfowl from fall into winter, depending upon the severity of the weather, and the shoreline is a great place to look for wading birds and shorebirds. The marshes have egrets and herons, and in summer and fall you can see willets, oystercatchers, and other marsh birds.

Other bayside trails include Tice's Shoal Coastal Heritage Trail near milepost 5 and Reed's Road Maritime Forest Trail just inside the main gate. This is the site of the former Reed's Hotel, which housed waterfowl hunters in the late 1800s and early 1900s, when Barnegat Bay was widely known among sportsmen.

Indeed, the human history of Barnegat Bay and Island Beach is as diverse and colorful as its natural history. The first known residents of Island Beach were the Lenape Indians, who were apparently seasonal visitors. They would come to catch fish, clams, oysters, and blue crabs, and they would gather gull and willet eggs, and trap muskrats and diamondback terrapins. They also would fashion wampum from the purple inner shell of the clam, which they would use in trade with inland tribes.

Henry Hudson's ship *Half Moon* anchored off Barnegat Inlet in 1609, and he and his crew explored the bay and the island. The ship's log notes that they found "many shoals" and a "great lake," and further noted that "this is a very good land to fall in with, and a pleasant place to see."

The first owner of Island Beach was apparently the first Earl of Sterling, who received a land grant from Charles I of England. Title to the land was passed down through his family, and by the time of the American Revolution it was in the hands of William Alexander, a descendant of the original earl. During the Revolution privateers sailed from Toms River and Tuckerton, preying on British shipping. Ships seized by this private navy, which was commissioned by the Continental Congress, were brought through Cranberry Inlet to Toms River or up Barnegat Inlet to Tuckerton, both of which were busy seaports in those days.

In the 1800s the maritime traditions drove the local economy with industries such as commercial fishing, trade, cargo transport, and passenger service. It was a dangerous business, though, especially in the vicinity of Barnegat Inlet, whose ever-changing shoals brought down many a ship. In the winter of 1826–1827, some two hundred ships were wrecked along the coast.

The specter of shipwrecks haunted a young local doctor, William Newell, who witnessed a wreck off Long Beach Island shortly after graduating from medical school. The loss of life seemed a needless tragedy to Newell, who later became a congressman and fought to pass legislation creating the United States Lifesaving Service. To Newell's great satisfaction, the service grew to include 271 stations, and its personnel were credited with saving more than 177,000 lives by the time the service was merged with the Revenue Cutter Service in 1915 to create the present day U.S. Coast Guard.

Although only ten thousand people lived in Ocean County in 1850, the area began to grow quickly after the Civil War when people who lived in Philadelphia, New York, and other cities discovered the pleasures of the ocean beach. Stagecoaches would transport visitors to the shore for 87½ cents, and boats sailed regularly for coastal resorts. In winter, the great flocks of waterfowl lured hunters from nearby cities, and hotels and lodges were built to accommodate them.

This early tourist industry was a boon to the local economy and helped establish the culture of the "baymen," local people who supported themselves entirely from the waters of Barnegat Bay. In summer they would catch fish, clams, diamondback terrapins, and crabs, which were shipped to restaurants and markets in the cities. In winter they hunted wildfowl for the market and guided visiting sportsmen who were willing to pay well for a successful week of duck hunting.

Island Beach came close to becoming another Jersey Shore resort in the late 1920s, but the development was stymied by the stock market crash of 1929. The island was purchased in 1926 by Henry Phipps, Andrew Carnegie's partner in Pittsburgh Steel. Phipps envisioned an upscale summer getaway for wealthy businessmen from eastern cities. Three homes were built before the market crash and resultant Depression ended Phipps's plan.

Through the 1930s and 1940s the most prominent name on the island was Francis Parkman Freeman, who had been hired by Phipps to be foreman of his Barnegat Bay and Beach Company. Freeman, his wife, and retired coast guard captain Joseph Tilton created the Borough of Island Beach, with Freeman serving as mayor and his wife as tax collector. They issued passes to visitors and administered the one hundred leases the company had issued to purchasers. Freeman was reportedly very protective of the island's wildlife. He instructed visitors to "leave things be, don't trample the sand dunes, don't pick the flowers, and don't annoy the osprey."

The island was evacuated during World War II, with the exception of the Freemans, who remained as caretakers. Following the war, the National Monument Committee attempted to purchase Island Beach for inclusion in the National Park Service, but Congress could not find sufficient funding. After several other failed attempts to save the island for the public good, the state of New Jersey was successful, as Governor Driscoll presented a check for $2.7 million to the heirs of Henry Phipps. During the brief ceremony, Governor Driscoll called Island Beach unique. "It is a jewel," he said. "There is nothing like it anywhere else on earth."

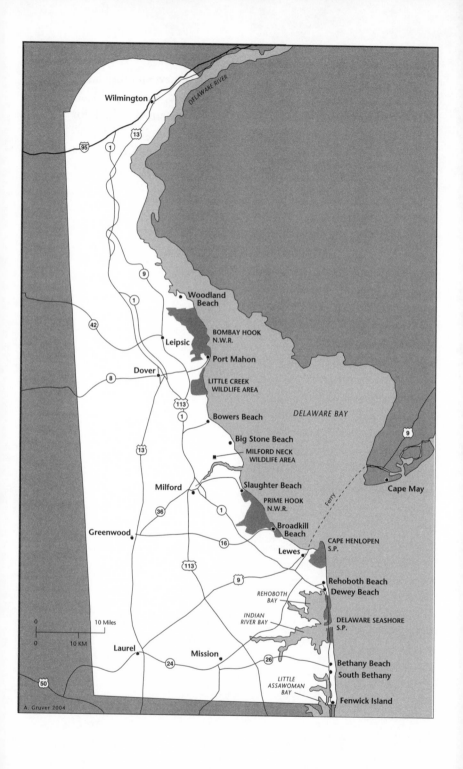

A. Gruver 2004

DELAWARE

A Lot of Coast, from Ocean to Bay

FOR A SMALL STATE, DELAWARE HAS SOME PRETTY IMPRES-
sive shoreline. It begins on the south at Fenwick Island, makes its
way northward along the Atlantic Ocean to South Bethany, Bethany Beach, Dewey Beach, and Rehoboth Beach. From there Delaware's coastline runs along Delaware Bay to Lewes, Slaughter
Beach, Bowers Beach, and on past Prime Hook, Bombay Hook,
Woodland Beach, and to Wilmington, at which point Delaware
Bay has become the Delaware River, dividing the states of New Jersey and Pennsylvania. It's an impressive watershed.

Along the ocean, the Delaware coast is a mixture of resort and
parkland. The towns have their share of hotels, restaurants, vacation rentals, and touristy shops, but Delaware Seashore State Park
offers an unbroken string of sandy beach, dunes, and shrub thickets that separate the ocean from the Rehoboth and Indian River
Bays. The park also includes Burton's Island at the Indian River
Marina, where an interpretive trail is located.

The Atlantic Ocean and Delaware Bay meet at Cape Henlopen,
a former military installation that today is a state park. The cape is
southeast of the historic town of Lewes (pronounced LOO-is), and
from the air it looks like an inverted comma, with a little curl of
sand jutting northward to define the two bodies of water. A breakwater and lighthouse lie just beyond the cape, protecting the port
of Lewes and the terminal where the Cape May–Lewes ferries dock.

The Delaware bayshore has seen little development, and much
of it is fringed by salt and brackish marsh. There are a few beach
communities—Slaughter Beach, Bowers, Fowler, Prime Hook,
Beach Plum Island, and Broadkill—but much of the southern
Delaware Bay shoreline is protected as Prime Hook or Bombay
Hook National Wildlife Refuge.

The Delaware Bay beaches, though, are becoming well known among birders, who arrive in late spring as horseshoe crabs migrate up the bay and come ashore to lay eggs above the high tide line. This is prime horseshoe crab habitat—sandy beach, gentle surf zone. More than half the North American population of red knots stops along the shores of Delaware Bay each spring.

There are several places along the bay to witness the shorebird migration, and to watch other birds during the various seasons. Follow state Road 16 east from U.S. Route 1 and you'll cross Prime Hook National Wildlife Refuge and end up at Broadkill Beach. A left turn along the way will take you to the refuge headquarters and visitor center, where there are hiking trails, a canoe trail, and helpful staff to provide information.

One of the best birding spots in the area is the shallow wetland along the causeway just west of the beach. A hard shoulder area provides off-road parking, and the ponds offer looks at various shorebirds and wading birds during spring and late summer, and waterfowl in the fall and winter.

Broadkill is essentially a residential community of summer homes, with Beach Plum State Park, south of the residential community, providing public access. A parking area is provided, and there are paths across the dunes to the beach, providing easy access for surf fishing and for those who simply want to explore the beach. It's an excellent venue for watching horseshoe crabs and shorebirds in May and early June.

The beaches here are narrow spits with a sandy berm, low dunes, and vegetated communities consisting of cedar, wild black cherry, bayberry, and beach plum. A wide expanse of marsh separates the beach from the mainland. Most of the marshland and contiguous upland are included in Prime Hook NWR.

Fowler Beach is a few miles north of Broadkill at the end of state Road 199 and is surrounded by Prime Hook NWR. The road provides a nice overlook of the salt marsh, including some stands of phragmites that are being reverted to *Spartina* marshes. The higher marsh has thick stands of marsh mallow, which adds a lot of color to the landscape in late summer. The road ends at the beach, with just enough room to turn around.

Slaughter Beach provides a good spot to observe shorebirds during the spring migration. In May and early June horseshoe crabs spawn on high tides, and shorebirds feed on the eggs at low tide. From fall to early spring waterfowl are present on the bay and in the marsh.

Milford Neck and Big Stone Beach are good places to watch shorebirds in spring and summer. You may see a variety of wading birds such as herons and egrets, shorebirds, rails and marsh sparrows, plus migrant songbirds in wooded areas. In fall, waterfowl, raptors, and migrating songbirds appear. Waterfowl and raptors often remain over winter.

Port Mahon, east of Dover, consists of farmland, forest, salt marsh, and bayshore. Much of it is protected, either by federal, state, or private conservation organizations. Bombay Hook NWR includes about 16,000 acres, and south of that is Little Creek Wildlife Area, which is owned by the state. The Nature Conservancy owns the 340-acre Port Mahon Preserve, at the end of state Road 8 on the Mahon River, a 1990 gift from Conectiv, the area's electricity and natural gas provider.

Woodland Beach is sandwiched between Bombay Hook National Wildlife Refuge and Woodland Beach Wildlife Area, which is managed by the state. It is a small beach community with a public launch ramp, fishing pier, and parking area. The pier provides a good look at the shoreline as well as the open water. Most of the shoreline here is peaty or lined with phragmites thickets, so it's not the best habitat for horseshoe crabs and shorebirds. The pier should provide a good view of sea ducks and other open-water birds in winter.

When it comes to open water, the Cape May–Lewes ferry is a great way to see Delaware Bay and a very pleasurable way of traveling between Delaware and New Jersey. The crossing takes less than two hours, the boats are clean and comfortable, and the views are outstanding. In fall and winter, sea ducks, pelagic species, and various waterfowl can be seen. Pods of bottlenose dolphins often swim alongside the ferry, and you can get a good look at both shorelines as the ferry nears the respective ports.

Delaware also has three shallow inland bays that are great for exploring and that also play an important role in the natural life of the coast. From north to south they are the Rehoboth Bay, the Indian River, and the Little Assawoman, which lies just over the Maryland line.

So the Delaware coast offers the Atlantic Ocean, Delaware Bay, three inland bays, and numerous rivers and creeks that meander far into the interior of the state. For a state of modest size, Delaware has a wealth of coastal resources.

Bombay Hook

On Delaware Bay, waterfowl gather by the thousands

We had nearly reached Bombay Hook when we saw smoke billowing over the trees in the distance. The smoke was white, and as it rose and then flattened and fell, we soon realized it was not smoke at all, but a billowing flock of geese, thousands of them, somewhere over Delaware Bay.

We had driven up Route 113 on the Eastern Shore, turned off on state Route 9 south of Dover, and then taken a two-lane roadway through farm country and river towns such as Little Creek and Leipsic. We stopped in Leipsic, bought Italian subs at the Leipsic Deli, and continued north to Whitehall Neck Road, which serves as the entrance to Bombay Hook National Wildlife Refuge.

Before we neared the refuge, we realized why Bombay Hook has earned a reputation as a magnet for waterfowl. The cornfields on both sides of the road had either snow geese, Canada geese, or tundra swans. We stopped the car, rolled down the windows, and listened. It was like a goose choir—some voices near and sharp, others distant and faint.

The swans were in small flocks of a few dozen birds, while the Canada geese traveled in packs of a hundred or more. The snow geese, though, were uncountable. They hung over the marshes of Bombay Hook Island in thick clouds, sometimes disappearing behind a stand of pines, but then reappearing just seconds later. Often a flock would break off and head for a mainland farm field, looking for a meal of winter wheat. But most stayed over the tidal marsh, rising and falling along the flats that separate the fastland from Delaware Bay.

Like most national wildlife refuges along the East Coast, Bombay Hook was created as a sanctuary for migrating waterfowl. The refuge was created in 1937 and is one of many of that particular vintage that provide a chain of rest stops in the Atlantic Flyway. The shallow freshwater pools and salt marshes attract tens of thousands of geese and ducks, many of which spend the winter here before heading north in the spring.

At nearly sixteen thousand acres, Bombay Hook is a large preserve, and today the constituency goes far beyond waterfowl. In summer the ponds and flats attract black-necked stilts, glossy ibises, herons, egrets, sandpipers, and other shorebirds and wading birds. The wooded sections provide an important migratory corridor for warblers, tanagers, and other neotropical migrant songbirds. The agricultural fields and grassy meadows attract sparrows, bluebirds, and indigo buntings among many others.

And of course there are the waterfowl. Snow geese gather in the marshes and fields in flocks of thousands. There are Canada geese, black ducks, mallards, and other dabbling ducks in the shallow pools, and the deeper tidal waters hold buffleheads, mergansers, loons, and other diving ducks.

Snow goose

There has long been human involvement in the marshes and fields of Bombay Hook. Native Americans and early settlers fished for crabs in the tidal creeks, gathered oysters and clams, and hunted waterfowl in winter. The first recorded history of the Bombay Hook area began in 1697, when Mechacksett, chief of the Kahansink, sold a tract of marshland to Peter Bayard of New York. Since then, salt hay has been harvested, fields planted, and dikes constructed.

The ponds at Bombay Hook were begun in the 1940s when Civilian Conservation Corps members based at nearby Leipsic built a series of dikes and water control structures. They were subsequently enlarged and improved upon, and now the refuge offers more than one thousand acres of freshwater pools and timbered swamps. The refuge also has some eleven hundred acres under cultivation, working with local farmers to produce crops that provide supplementary feed to waterfowl and other migrating birds. A major portion of the refuge is occupied by forest and by vast expanses of pristine salt marsh, one of the most valuable natural areas in the Delaware Bay area.

Bombay Hook NWR covers a sizeable portion of the bayshore in Delaware. Refuge property begins along the Mahon River on the south and includes Kelly, Kent, and Bombay Hook Islands, along with the marshes of Simons and Leipsic Rivers and Duck Creek. The sluice ditch east of Bear Swamp Pool is the northern boundary. The refuge covers about eight miles of shoreline on the bay.

If you're unfamiliar with the refuge, the visitor center should be your first stop. There you can pick up a refuge map, guides to the trails, and an auto tour brochure. Most people see the refuge by car, which is something of a shame, because there are several good hiking paths and wooded areas that are full of warblers in spring and fall. The car does come in handy in summer, though, because the twelve miles of road are hot and dusty, and there's a good chance the insects will be out in force. Mosquitos and greenhead flies can make life miserable for pedestrians during the warm months, so be forewarned.

The refuge lends itself well to bicycle tours in spring and fall, when the weather is cooperative and the bugs are dormant. The bike is a good compromise between the car, which makes you miss a lot of good stuff, and hiking, which can get tiring if you plan to cover all twelve miles of roads plus the side trails. So if the weather is amenable, bring the bike, and if it's not, drive the family van, but stop for the hiking trails and linger over the freshwater impoundments with the binoculars and spotting scope.

The most accessible portions of the refuge are near the pools. The roadway, much of which runs atop an earthen dike, provides access to the best birding and botanizing sections of Bombay Hook. From the visitor center the road forks off to the right and makes a circle around Raymond Pool. A Boardwalk Trail, for hikers only, branches off the road, circles a small pond, and offers a great lookout over the salt marshes and a tidal gut that empties into the Leipsic River. (In seaside taxonomy, a gut is narrower than a creek but wider than a ditch.) This short trail is a good place to look for songbirds, especially when the warblers are moving through in spring and fall.

The road continues north along Shearness Pool, which will be on your left, and the tidal salt marsh. A right turn will take you around Bear Swamp Pool, which usually has numerous shorebirds and a great concentration of black-crowned night herons. Bear Swamp Trail is a productive short hike for migratory songbirds or resident birds, although if the weather has been wet, you'll need boots.

Once around Bear Swamp Pool, you can turn right and exit the refuge via Dutch Neck Road, or you can drive down to Finis Pool, which in most seasons is a good idea. The wetlands, woods, and open meadows offer many different species of birds, depending upon the time of year. The pool here is fed by a freshwater stream, and the four hundred acres of woods nearby have been left largely undisturbed. So what we have here is a freshwater habitat suitable to a wide range of plants and animals. The woods has some of the largest trees on the refuge—sweet gum, white oak, and black tupelo—and the plants include jack-in-the-pulpit and pink lady slipper, which blooms in May. The woods is perhaps the best location on the refuge to watch migrating songbirds in the spring and summer.

While the pools and trails are the most obvious places to explore, don't overlook the upland areas of the refuge, including the cultivated fields. Geese and other waterfowl use these tracts extensively in winter, and there is always the chance to pick out a rarity—a Ross's goose, perhaps, well hidden among all of those snow geese.

The upland fields provide good birding in late summer and early spring, when the shorebirds are moving through. If the weather has been wet and the fields are saturated and have standing water, check the birds out with the spotting scope.

Most people who visit Bombay Hook NWR come for the birds. The official "Bombay Hook list," published and updated regularly by the refuge, names 267 birds that have been identified on the refuge. What makes Bombay Hook so attractive to so many birds? If you checked "habitat" on your score sheet, give yourself an "A."

In its sixteen thousand acres, Bombay Hook has bayshore beach, tidal salt marsh, brackish ponds, fresh ponds, hardwood swamps, shallow pools, streams, cultivated land, undisturbed meadows, upland forest, and deep, fast-moving saltwater creeks and tidal rivers.

Whatever a bird is looking for, Bombay Hook probably has it, at least during part of the year.

There really is no off-season when it comes to birding at Bombay Hook. Even in summer, after the spring movement of shorebirds and warblers, and prior to their return in August, there are birds to see. The pools will likely be shallow and reduced in acreage, but if you stay for a while along the edges and patiently scan the flats and wetted areas with binoculars, you're likely to see glossy ibises, black-necked stilts, avocets, semi-palmated sandpipers, least sandpipers, killdeer, yellowlegs, black-crowned night herons, great blue herons, and great and snowy egrets. It's not uncommon to see a half dozen black-crowned night herons perched in a deadfall along Bear Swamp Pool on a July day.

Fall brings the great flocks of waterfowl, for which the refuge is best known. The flights depend upon the weather, beginning in September with teal and continuing through the winter with the arrival of thousands of snow geese. These are the star attractions of Bombay Hook in the minds of most visitors. After all, who wouldn't be moved by the sight of thousands of snow geese, moving like a cloud against a blue sky, singing in harmony, coming to rest in a field of winter wheat?

But fall brings other visitors to Bombay Hook. The shorebirds resume their migration in August, and the neotropical migrant songbirds begin coming through in late August and early September. The songbird migration will continue until November, as great flocks of yellow-rumped warblers gather in the myrtles and bayberry bushes. Most songbirds nest in the northern United States and Canada and travel to South and Central America for the winter. As they travel, the forested corridor along Delaware Bay provides food, rest, and protection from predators. A few songbirds actually nest here, including the red-eyed vireo, yellow warbler, and common yellowthroat. Only the yellow-rumped warbler is found in large numbers in the winter.

Spring is something of a mirror image of fall, but more colorful and more musical. The male songbirds are in their best nuptial attire, and they sing regularly, either to attract a mate, to stake out territory, or to warn off other males. Most people who enjoy songbirds enjoy the spring season because the birds can be identified by song or by plumage. The migration begins as early as March and runs into May.

The spring migration of shorebirds is also a big draw, and although there is no easily accessed beachfront on Bombay Hook, the freshwater pools are usually very productive for spotting a variety of sandpipers, plovers, turnstones, and other species.

The current bird list published by the refuge is handy in that it not only names the seasons when the birds are most prevalent, but it also gives their preferred habitat. Part of the fun of studying birds is learning not only what they look like, but also how they act, what type of habitat they prefer, and in whose company they are most likely to be found. This aspect of the guide is invaluable, leading visitors toward areas where they are most likely to see the birds they are seeking.

Cape Henlopen

A sandy search for a snowy owl goes unrewarded

Three years ago I nearly stepped on a snowy owl on the beach at
Cape Henlopen State Park. I was walking with my head down,
looking for something interesting in the sand, when the owl and I
surprised each other. I thought at first it was an old white garbage
bag sitting there, and then it lifted a wing. I don't know what the
owl thought.

Unfortunately, that was the last time I saw a snowy owl, much
less stepped on one. So on a long winter weekend my wife and I
decided to go back and see if there were still any owls on that
beach. Lynn and our son, Tom, had never seen one, and she was
keen to add one to her life list. Tom was sixteen at the time and sat
in the backseat and read *Guitar World*.

Cape Henlopen is shaped like an upside-down comma. The little tail of the comma sticks out in Delaware Bay, separating it from
the Atlantic Ocean, so you can walk down one side of the comma
on the bay and return on the other side, along the ocean. The
little tip of the comma is a good place to find snowy owls.

One thing we hadn't anticipated when we left home was that
the wind was going to be blowing out of the north around forty
knots, right in our faces as we hiked toward the point. This not
only made things uncomfortable, but it also made visibility very
poor. Fine sand hung in the air like a morning mist, a thick, abra-
sive cloud. If I had been watching this scene on TV, no doubt it
would have been lovely—sand skittering across the spit, piling up
in wind shadows behind the dunes, sunlight breaking through
clouds in golden shafts.

I leaned into the wind and wished I'd brought my duck hunting clothes instead of the Barbour jacket, which is very nice as long
as it's not windy. Lynn and I pressed on, looking for old white

garbage bags that sometimes moved. We scoured the beach with the binoculars and peered into the dunes as best we could. (They're closed to hikers to prevent damage to vegetation.) Tom actually seemed to be having a good time. He had brought along our new digital camera and was photographing the sunlight breaking through the clouds, casting shadows on the dunes.

We made it to the tip, hiked along the ocean side, and realized that on this particular day we were unlikely to see a snowy owl. On the way back, we had the wind behind us.

Cape Henlopen State Park has more to offer than snowy owls, so we decided to explore. The park is among the oldest public lands in America. William Penn, in 1682, declared that the lands of the cape were for the common use of the citizens of Lewes and Sussex Counties, thus establishing the nation's first public parks. Cape Henlopen served as a military base during World War II, and for centuries the old lighthouse and breakwater provided guidance and safe harbor for sailors.

The military presence is easily recognized today. Most of the park roads are of World War II–vintage concrete. Bunkers and former gun emplacements are tucked into dunes and bluffs, and concrete lookout towers provide a sweeping view of the entrance to Delaware Bay. A former barracks has been renovated and is now used as an environmental education center.

In summer the big draw here is the ocean beach, and the campground is usually filled with vacationing families. In winter and early spring, the park gets weekend hikers and bicyclists. There are several miles of paved bike paths, one of which leads to the top of a bluff overlooking the ocean, presenting a view well worth the uphill grind.

Birders flock to the park in April and May to witness the annual horseshoe crab and shorebird phenomenon. The crabs lumber ashore on the bay side of the spit to lay eggs, and the birds will soon follow, feasting on the eggs as they travel to breeding grounds in the Arctic.

The nature center near the park entrance is a good place to begin a trip to Cape Henlopen. Books, maps, and brochures are available, and interpretive displays provide a look at the bay/ocean ecosystem of the cape. Information is also available on programs and nature tours led by staff naturalists.

Our most recent visit to Cape Henlopen did not produce a snowy owl, but if the bird were commonplace and easy to find, it wouldn't be special. The snowy owl carries a certain aura of mystery and intrigue. It is a large white owl that spends most of its life on the open tundra of the Arctic, preying chiefly on lemmings. In the dead of winter, when the lemming population ebbs, the birds sometimes retreat from their northern range, a move necessitated by hunger. That's when we have a chance to see them.

"Look at it this way," said Lynn. "It's disappointing not to see a snowy owl, but from the birds' point of view, the fact that they're not here is probably good news."

※ ※ ※

Cape Henlopen is just south of Lewes, an old port town that has a colorful history. For those who like boats and the water, it's a good place to spend a day, walking the narrow streets, prowling around the harbor, looking for bargains in shops.

Lewes was settled in 1631 by the Dutch, who thought the cape would make a good whaling station. The early days of Lewes did not go smoothly. The Lenape Indians had already established residence in the area, and in a dispute over a coat of arms the Indians killed thirty-two settlers. In 1682 the land was conveyed to William Penn, who gave the settlement the name it has today in honor of a town in Sussex County, England.

Lewes was a target of pirates in the early 1700s, and in 1812 it was bombed by a British frigate. One of the buildings in town, appropriately named Cannonball House, still has a cannon round embedded in its wall.

Lewes is considerably more peaceful today. There have been no massacres or attacks by the British navy in recent memory. The one constant, though, has been the water. Lewes has always been a seafaring town, and so it is today. The harbor has a large fleet of fishing boats, and it is the home base of the Delaware Bay and

River Pilots Association, whose members guide cargo vessels to and from ports in Wilmington and Philadelphia. The ferry to Cape May departs from a terminal just south of town, and the University of Delaware has its College of Marine Studies in Lewes.

Sussex County has grown tremendously in recent years. Delaware Route 1, the north-south highway that gets all of those tourists to the beaches, once ran through farm fields and pinewoods. Today there are outlet malls, motels, restaurants, and shopping centers. Lewes, which is just off Route 1, is like a peaceful little island, a place to escape to after you've bought your four pairs of designer jeans at thrift shop prices. It's the eye in a storm of traffic and congestion.

While Route 1 is centered on the motor vehicle, Lewes encourages visitors to park the car and explore on foot. A municipal lot is conveniently located right at the waterfront, convenient to all of those shops and restaurants on Front Street and Second Street. Most of the buildings here are old, and it pays to pry around alleyways and basement entrances. I found a wonderful gallery that specializes in art photography in a little basement nook next door to a restaurant. An alleyway adjacent to another restaurant leads to an antiques shop and a small cluster of restored merchants buildings and sea pilots' homes.

The most eye-catching building in town is the Zwaanendael Museum, which was built in 1931 to commemorate the three-hundredth anniversary of the first European settlement in Delaware. The museum is made of carved stonework with an ornamented gable and is adapted from the old town hall in Hoorn, Holland. Inside there are displays and artifacts that feature the seafaring past of Lewes and Sussex County, including some pieces found in the shipwrecked brig *DeBraak,* which went down off Lewes in 1798.

Lewes even has a public beach. I drove down Savannah Road, crossed the Lewes-Rehoboth Canal, passed several motels that cater to visiting fishermen, and soon had my feet in the sand. In the distance was the Lewes harbor, with one of the big ferries heading off toward Cape May. There were containerships passing in the bay, as well as a few fishermen going after striped bass and gray trout. Somewhere in the distance was the New Jersey shore and the Cape May Lighthouse. As I looked for its blinking light on the far shore, dolphins broke the calm water just off the beach, moving in and out of the water without creating a splash.

The Inland Bays

Taking the pulse of the estuary

The waters of Indian River Bay are full of life, and we wanted to find out just what sorts of tiny animals are swimming around out there. Captain Larry Karpinski cranked down the throttle of the *Sand Dollar,* and we began a plankton tow, slowly pulling behind us a fine mesh net that looks like a weather vane with a jar attached to the small end. A sinker attached to a line just ahead of the large end keeps everything just under water, and as we slowly moved along, the net scooped up everything in its way and dispatched it to the collecting jar at the rear.

After a few minutes Kristel Sharman tugged on the line, lifted the net aboard, and detached the jar. She held it to the sun and examined the contents. There were bits and pieces of grass and other nonliving material, but there were also dozens of tiny marine creatures just barely large enough for the unaided eye to see. Kristel transferred some of the water to a container with a magnifying lid, and we soon recognized tiny shrimp, crab larvae, fish larvae, and many other animals we could not possibly identify.

"I've spent many hours on Indian River Bay, but this job has given me a new appreciation for the richness of this ecosystem, for the amount of life it supports," said Kristel. Kristel and her friend Colleen Schilly have what might be the perfect summer jobs. They work for the Delaware Division of Parks and Recreation, and their job is to monitor the health of Delaware's inland bays and to do so with an audience. Their stage is the *Sand Dollar,* a pontoon boat large enough to accommodate a crowd of tourists but with a sufficiently shallow draft that it can navigate the shallow waters of Indian River and Rehoboth Bays. Kristel, who lives in nearby Georgetown, is a junior at Gordon College in Massachusetts. Colleen is a junior at Duke University. Both are majoring in environmental science.

The *Sand Dollar* sails twice a day, Wednesday through Friday, from the Indian River marina. On the two-hour morning cruise Kristel and Colleen measure salinity, check for dissolved oxygen and nitrates, check turbidity, and collect various fish and shellfish from larval stage to mature adult. Passengers are encouraged not only to watch but to get their hands muddy too. All the while, visitors are gently reminded how rich with life is this shallow estuary, how fragile, how important it is that we protect it.

Delaware has three inland bays: the Rehoboth, Indian River, and Little Assawoman Bay, near the Maryland line. The bays are very shallow, which makes them extremely productive because sunlight easily penetrates to the bottom. Captain Larry, as he welcomes everyone aboard, notes that the life jackets, should we need them, are stored in the overhead compartments. "But if you fall overboard," says Larry, "the best thing to do is just walk back to the boat. The average depth outside the channels is about three feet."

The three bays drain most of southeastern Delaware. Indian River flows all the way up to Millsboro on U.S. Route 113. Countless other streams flow through farmland and forest and empty into the bays, bringing with them soil sediments and whatever might be attached to them. The coast is heavily developed, but once you get off the main roads, you'll find that Delaware is still essentially a rural state, where grain farming and chicken production are major industries. Threats to the bays are mainly non–point sources of pollution: fertilizers from farm fields, poultry wastes, runoff from chemically enhanced lawns, and petrochemicals washed by rains from highways and parking lots. "The most popular forms of recreation here used to be fishing and going to the beach. Now it's going to the outlet malls," Colleen tells us. "That means more cars, more highways, more parking lots, more people driving."

Despite the development, Indian River Bay seems to be in good shape. A test for nitrates turned out negative, meaning that at least for that particular time and place, there was no evidence that chemical runoff was a problem. Indeed, the bay seemed to be teeming with life. An Amish family had anchored their boat in the shallows and were wading for clams, the women wearing white bonnets and full-length dresses. Other boats were drifting along the channel edge, fishing for flounder and weakfish. We pulled a crab trap and found numerous blue crabs, a staple of the commercial fishery in summer. Our trap had several "sponge crabs," females with a mass of yellow eggs bulging beneath the apron on their abdomen. On the beach at Burton's Island dozens of horseshoe crabs had laid their eggs and died. Flocks of gulls hovered over the beach, some landing to feed on the crabs or on the eggs they had deposited by the millions on the sand. Shorebirds had fed on the eggs and were now on their way to nesting areas in the Arctic, leaving the feast to the laughing gulls and herring gulls.

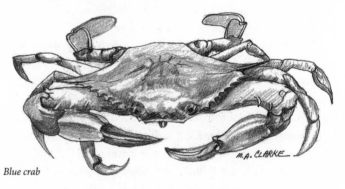

Blue crab

The inland bays of Delaware are hard-working protein factories, churning out great masses of fish and shellfish, some in adult stage, some as eggs and larvae. In early summer, the water is clouded with tiny plants, called phytoplankton, and animals, called zooplankton. Kristel dropped a Secchi disc overboard, which is used to measure the turbidity of water. The disc is about the size of a dinner plate and painted with a bold black-and-white pattern. The line attached to the disc has markings at one-foot increments, and as Kristel slowly lowered the disc, the pattern grew faint and disappeared from view at a depth of about three feet, meaning that the water was carrying a lot of suspended material.

"People see that the water here is murky and they assume it's polluted, or carrying a lot of sediment, but plant and animal life are making the water cloudy," says Kristel. "People go to the Caribbean and see the crystal blue water down there and think it's beautiful, but the water we have here in the Delaware bays is much more alive. The water here is carrying millions of living things."

The living things suspended in the water include tiny plants, which mainly are in the upper portions to reach sunlight, and animals, many of which will one day play an important role in the economy of Sussex County. There are tiny fish, blue crab and shrimp larvae, clam eggs and larvae, and the larvae of horseshoe crabs.

These shallow bays are a productive nursery, and as long as the nursery is protected and its health maintained, it will continue to churn out this great mass of life. Taking its pulse is an important job. Colleen takes a sample of bay water, tests it for nitrogen, and is pleased that the test shows low levels. "We need nitrogen for life, but too much of it can be harmful," she says. "Nitrogen occurs naturally in the environment, but a surplus can come from fertilizer, animal waste, sewage plants, and fossil fuel combustion. Too much nitrogen causes massive plant growth, and the plants rob the water of oxygen and can cause fish kills and other problems. It's a case of too much of a good thing being bad for you."

❊ ❊ ❊

The James Farm is a scenic slice of Cedar Neck, a 150-acre cross-section of a finger of land that pokes out into Indian River Bay. You can walk from one end of the farm to the other and get a great view of the bay at each end. Ed Lewandowski is the education and outreach coordinator for the Delaware Center for the Inland Bays, a nonprofit group whose mission is to educate people about the inland bays and to restore and protect them. The center's keystone project is the James Farm, which was donated to Sussex County by the late Mary Lighthipe. In deeding the land to the county, Mrs. Lighthipe specified that the tract could be used for environmental education and recreation, but construction of permanent facilities was prohibited. The center began managing the farm in 1998 under an occupancy agreement with the county.

To Ed Lewandowski, the farm is an open-air classroom, a place where people can come to explore salt marshes, walk on the beach, or hike trails that wind through hardwood forests, meadows, and ancient maritime dune thickets. The farm is next door to Delaware Seashore State Park, so what we have here are several hundred acres of protected land set amid the fastest-growing piece of real estate in Delaware. It is an island of green and quiet in an area where soybean fields are quickly giving way to subdivisions.

Although permanent buildings are not allowed on the preserve, hiking trails, viewing platforms, and an amphitheater have been constructed. It's a popular destination for science teachers at local high schools, a place where students can see and feel what they read about in textbooks.

From a platform on the western side of the farm, Burton's Island can be seen in the distance. In early summer a second small island nearby becomes a heronry, a noisy and busy place where breeding birds seek safety in numbers. It's called Middle Island, and it consists of about two acres of salt marsh, a small sandy beach, and a few pine snags on a narrow rim of upland. When we visited, each pine had a woody nest occupied by a great blue heron, and there were a few dozen snowy egrets, little blue herons, oystercatchers, and other nesting birds. To the right is the Indian River Inlet bridge and U.S. Route 1, which heads north up the barrier island to Dewey Beach.

There is a sandy beach here, a promising place to look for clams, but most of the fringe is salt marsh, great meadows of *Spartina alterniflora*, the predominant plant of these salty lowlands. This is one of Ed Lewandowski's favorite outdoor classrooms. "We have a great diversity of plant life in a relatively compact area," he says. "So you can bring students here and show them the beach, the marsh, the fringe, and the upland and show them the different plants that are common to each area. We can stand here and see *spartina* marshes, thickets of wax myrtle in slightly higher areas, and then the mixed hardwood forest and even a little maritime forest. Years ago the forests here were dunes, and the soil is very sandy. So we can show students a wide range of plant communities in a small area."

The Center for the Inland Bays has four missions: research, education, restoration, and public policy. All are addressed in one way or another at the James Farm Ecological Preserve. Research and restoration are ongoing processes, ranging from aquaculture to submerged aquatic vegetation. Ed pointed out white PVC pipes outlining an area just off the beach. "We transplanted eelgrass from Chincoteague Bay to Indian River Bay, and it seems to be doing well here," he says. "The bay is shallow, and at one time eelgrass was very prevalent, and a lot of small fish and shellfish lived in eelgrass beds. If we can restore the beds, we can improve the habitat for these marine animals as well. The center has also constructed oyster reefs and experimented with clam aquaculture, and we're converting the upland fields back to a mixed hardwood forest."

The center's fourth mission, public policy, is the goal of the first three. The center was established by the state to develop a long-term approach for the wise use and enhancement of the inland bays watershed, and the James Farm is a model, demonstrating that decisions made by state and local governments have a certain and lasting effect. Development also has such an effect. A few miles away, shopping centers, outlet malls, and restaurants cover what once was a barrier beach. Even at the James Farm, new subdivisions are going in next door. Houses are being built on land that still bears the stubble of last year's soybean crop. We walked the farm and enjoyed the quiet, but left unanswered were the questions: Is it enough? And is it too late?

Limulus Visits Broadkill

A tradition lives on

On a spring evening at Broadkill Beach, a formidable-looking brown creature slowly emerged from the waters of Delaware Bay and made its way up the berm of the beach. And then came another. And another. Within an hour, the narrow beach had become nearly covered, and yet others swam clumsily in the shallow water, rocked by waves that broke onshore.

These creatures were horseshoe crabs, and they were in the process of laying eggs, beginning a spring ritual that has gone on for hundreds of years. The crabs would deposit tens of millions of eggs on Broadkill Beach, but only a tiny fraction of them would ever be fertilized and grow to adulthood. Even as the crabs laid their eggs, great flocks of birds gathered—sandpipers, plovers, red knots, turnstones, dowitchers—and the birds feasted on the crab eggs, plucking some from the surface of the sand, probing for buried ones with their beaks.

These shorebirds were travelers, on their way to the Arctic from wintering grounds in South America. They would spend two to three weeks on the shores of Delaware Bay, resting and replenishing energy reserves before resuming their trip. The horseshoe crabs had just provided them with their primary source of fuel.

On the coast, the process of breeding and reproduction is not simply a matter of maintaining the population of a species. A female clam will produce thousands of eggs, but very few are destined to become adult clams. Instead, clam eggs and larvae are the building blocks of the salt marsh food chain, feeding the countless fish and shellfish that share the estuary. And so it is with horseshoe crabs; the process of laying and fertilizing eggs has implications much broader than simply creating a new horseshoe crab to replace an aging one. It is a splendid example of how nature is interconnected, how species depend upon one another for health and well-being.

The horseshoe crab, *Limulus polyphemus,* is not a crab at all, but is more closely related to the trilobites, which existed more than five hundred million years ago. Scientists say the animal is virtually untouched by evolution; the current incarnation harkens back to the Silurian period, when land animals first evolved. To some eyes they are fearsome creatures; large females can grow to much more than a foot in diameter, and the spiked tail would appear to be a formidable weapon. But horseshoe crabs are harmless, slow-moving animals that play a vital role in the dynamics of the coast, and that dangerous-looking tail is used to right the crab should it capsize in the surf.

The Delaware estuary is the largest staging area for shorebirds in the Atlantic Flyway, with as many as one million birds converging on the area in mid to late May. The horseshoe crab is crucial to the bird migration because the great mass of eggs are produced just as the birds are entering the region. The crabs are drawn to Delaware Bay because, for the most part, the shoreline provides the proper environment for egg laying. The crabs are looking for a porous, sandy beach, well oxygenated, where the eggs can develop and survive predators. They want a beach that is somewhat protected from heavy surf; after all, they have to swim through it numerous times. What the crabs don't want is a hard, peaty shoreline or one that has been altered by the addition of bulkheads and groins. There still are plenty of sandy beaches on the Delaware and New Jersey shores, and this sandy shoreline, sparsely populated by humans, is ideal horseshoe crab habitat.

While horseshoe crabs fuel the migration of hundreds of thousands of birds, their eggs and larvae feed a wide range of other animals as well, including striped bass and other finfish, eels, crabs, whelks, sea turtles, and various invertebrates. The crabs also host many marine creatures. Crabs grow by shedding old shells and developing new, larger replacements, but as crabs age they shed less often and thus pick up various hitchhikers, which attach them-

Horseshoe crabs

selves to the shell. If you look closely at a large crab you may find barnacles, anemones, tube worms and scale worms, algae, oyster drills and other snails, jingle shells, starfish, sponges, leeches, small oysters and mussels, and slipper shells, as well as eggs and larvae of numerous species.

Scientists say horseshoe crabs are virtually unchanged since the time land animals developed. The crabs belong to the phylum *arthropoda*, which includes insects, spiders, and crustaceans. Horseshoe crabs belong to neither of those classes, though, and instead occupy one of their own, called *Merostomata*, which means "legs attached to the mouth." While there are millions of species of insects worldwide, and thousands of species of arachnids and crustaceans, only four species of *Merostomata* exist. The horseshoe crab of Delaware Bay and the Atlantic Coast is *Limulus polyphemus*. The other three species are found in the Indian and Pacific Oceans.

Horseshoe crabs spawn in Delaware Bay in May and June, with the peak occurring on evening high tides during the full and new moons. When the crabs come ashore, the males will patrol the shallow water at the foot of the beach. As the females approach and make their way ashore, they give off chemical attractants called pheromones, which the males detect. The males, which are smaller than the females, attach themselves to their mate with a claw they use to grasp the female's back. During the peak of spawning time, a single female may have a group of four or five males huddled around her.

Prior to spawning, the female will develop a mass of some eighty thousand eggs near the front of her shell. The eggs are laid on successive high tides in four or five clutches of four thousand eggs each. Each female will lay about twenty clusters of eggs per year. As each cluster of eggs is deposited, it is fertilized by the male crab, which attaches itself to the female with pincers and emits milts sperm as the female's eggs are being released. Scientists believe that the most viable eggs are those deposited at some depth in the sand, thus protecting them from predators. So those eaten by birds likely would not have survived anyway.

The eggs hatch in about fourteen days, with those in warmer sand higher on the beach developing sooner. The crab larvae return to the bay, and as they grow they move to deeper waters. The young crabs molt several times during their first few years, with the periods between molts becoming longer as the crab grows larger. Male crabs will molt about sixteen times by the time they reach sexual maturity at age nine. The larger females will not reach sexual maturity until their eleventh year, when they begin their annual spawning migration back to the beaches.

The chances of a horseshoe crab egg surviving to become a breeding adult are similar to those of winning a lottery. The egg must become fertilized, develop into a larva, return to the open sea, and then, over eleven years of molts, develop into a breeding adult. And then she must swim back into the estuary, find a suitable beach, and lay the eighty thousand eggs as her mother had done. It is remarkable that it can happen. What's even more remarkable is that horseshoe crabs apparently have the same homing instinct as salmon and striped bass, in that they seek out their natal estuary. So the crabs you see at Broadkill Beach were likely raised from eggs laid nearby more than ten years ago.

Horseshoe crabs have more to worry about than migrating shorebirds. While the birds consume prodigious quantities of eggs, scientists believe they pose no threat to the crab because of the sheer number of eggs produced. More troublesome is the mortality of adult crabs, especially females, each of which can produce tens of thousands of eggs per year.

According to the Ecological Research and Development Group (ERDG) of Lewes, Delaware, a nonprofit organization formed in 1995 to conserve the world's four species of horseshoe crabs, millions of crabs are killed each year to be used as bait in the eel and whelk fishery. More die because their blood is used in the medical industry to detect bacterial contamination. Although crabs are returned to the water after giving blood, the mortality rate is still estimated at 10 to 15 percent. The increasing commercial use of crabs has prompted many states to pass stricter bag limits on commercial fishing.

The problem, according to ERDG, is that no one seems to know how many horseshoe crabs are on the mid–Atlantic Coast. Conservative estimates put the population at 2.3 to 4.5 million crabs between Virginia and New Jersey. Other estimates are higher. Although there have been horseshoe crab censuses done over the years, the methods have been inconsistent, and so there is no baseline, no data to indicate whether the population today is higher or lower than it was ten or twenty years ago.

One thing we do know is that for the last few years, the horseshoe crabs have returned to the sands of Broadkill Beach, but their numbers have been fewer. Are they going elsewhere? Are their habits being changed by weather patterns? Or are there simply fewer horseshoe crabs around today than ten years ago?

MARYLAND

The Chesapeake Is in the Blood

THINK CRAB CAKES AT A DOCKSIDE RESTAURANT, SAILING ON an open bay, casting lures for rockfish, canoeing a tidal creek, eagles soaring over a salt marsh, Canada geese flocking to fields of cutover corn. The Maryland coast is all this and more. From the Atlantic resort of Ocean City to quiet coves along the Chesapeake Bay, Maryland offers something for most tastes and desires.

Ocean City is a busy resort town, and the "wildest" element here would probably be the nightlife between Memorial Day and Labor Day. The southern part of the beach town is the original Ocean City resort, with its wooden boardwalk, sturdy frame hotels with wide porches facing the ocean, and arcades and rides and the world's best french fries. The northern part of the city is newer, and the architecture shows it. High-rise condominiums, hotels, and shopping centers are the order of the day.

While Ocean City is highly developed, those of us seeking more natural attractions still have reason to visit the resort. A walk on the beach is especially enjoyable in winter, when seabirds are gliding in ragged strings just beyond the breakers. A boat trip offshore will usually turn up various pelagic bird species, and the bays that separate Ocean City from the mainland are also good spots to look for birds.

But to find a beach with a more natural appeal, it will be necessary to go a bit farther south, cross the inlet, and visit Assateague Island. Assateague is a large island, reaching well into Virginia, and it can be accessed by the Verrazano Bridge, near the town of Berlin, or via the town of Chincoteague, Virginia. The inlet that separates Ocean City and Assateague was created by a hurricane in 1933, and in the 1950s a major residential development was planned for Assateague, with nine thousand building lots being laid out. The

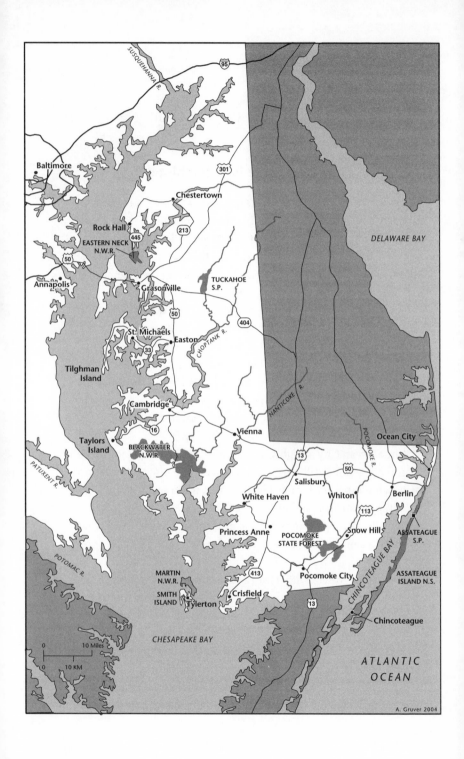

SUSQUEHANNA R.

95

Baltimore

301

Chestertown

Rock Hall
445
EASTERN NECK
N.W.R.

213

50

Annapolis

Grasonville

TUCKAHOE
S.P.

DELAWARE BAY

50

St. Michaels
33
Easton

404

CHOPTANK R.

Tilghman
Island

NANTICOKE R.

Cambridge
16
Vienna

POCOMOKE R.

Taylors
Island

BLACKWATER
N.W.R.

Ocean City

PATUXENT R.

13

Salisbury
50

White Haven
Whiton
Berlin

Princess Anne
113

Snow Hill
ASSATEAGUE
S.P.

POCOMOKE
STATE FOREST

POTOMAC R.

MARTIN
N.W.R.

413

CHINCOTEAGUE BAY

ASSATEAGUE
ISLAND N.S.

SMITH
ISLAND
Tylerton
Crisfield

Pocomoke City

13

Chincoteague

0   10 Miles
0   10 KM

CHESAPEAKE BAY

ATLANTIC
OCEAN

A. Gruver 2004

March storm of 1962 ended those plans, and the island today is
made up of a state park, national seashore, and national wildlife
refuge.

Most of Maryland's coast fronts the Chesapeake Bay, and with
it hundreds of rivers, creeks, and streams that meander far into the
body of the state. Baltimore boasts a major commercial port, and
Annapolis is the capital of recreational boating, but most of Maryland's bay country consists of vast salt marsh meadows, farm
fields, and small towns tied to the pulse of the bay. Places like
Tilghman Island are still working watermen's towns, where the
growl of diesel engines aboard bayboats starts the day. When oysters were plentiful, skipjacks would sail out of Tilghman and
dredge bushels of oysters by mid-morning. In summer fishermen
would catch blue crabs and fish for the market. Diseases have dec-
imated the oyster population, but crabbing is still a viable industry, and a growing recreational fishing industry is keeping mari-
nas, motels, and guides busy.

The Maryland bayshore has a wealth of protected lands, including national wildlife refuges, state forests and wildlife management
areas, as well as private preserves such as the Nature Conservancy's
Nassawango Creek Preserve and the Pickering Creek Environmental Center, which is operated by the Chesapeake Audubon Society.

Maryland's Eastern Shore offers a wealth of natural diversity.
Thousands of acres are protected by the state as Pocomoke River
State Forest, where extensive cypress forests provide breeding habitat for prothonotary warblers, woodpeckers, vireos, and many other
species. The Nature Conservancy owns a seventy-two-hundred-
acre preserve along Nassawango Creek, a tributary of the Pocomoke, where a day spent in a canoe can turn up all sorts of birding and botanical gems.

Blackwater National Wildlife Refuge, near Cambridge, has
twenty-three thousand acres of marsh and impoundments that
attract great flocks of ducks and geese, as well as bald eagles. The
refuge has the largest nesting population on the East Coast north
of Florida, and there is a chance of seeing golden eagles in winter.

A wide variety of other birds are found on the refuge year-round, especially herons, waterfowl, raptors, and shorebirds. Breeding species include black-necked stilts, summer tanagers, blue grosbeaks, grasshopper sparrows, chuck-will's-widows, and brown-headed nuthatches. Endangered Delmarva fox squirrels are present throughout the year.

Drive the back roads near Easton in the fall, or head up to Chestertown and out to Rock Hall, and in nearly every mile you'll see Canada geese hanging over cornfields in uneven lines. Stop the car, roll down the window, and listen to the goose music; it chills the spine, a harbinger of winter. Waterfowl hunting has long been a winter tradition in Maryland, a part of the culture of Eastern Shore communities. Easton's Waterfowl Festival, held each November, is a nationally known festival of the hunting tradition and wildlife art.

Pickering Creek Environmental Center is just outside Easton and is a good place to visit for those of us who like to look for birds. You'll see waterfowl in fall and winter, but spring and early fall bring great concentrations of songbirds, such as warblers, vireos, tanagers, and thrushes, which move through the forested areas as they migrate between winter homes in the tropics and breeding grounds in the Arctic. The Pickering Creek center includes four hundred acres of woodland, upland, and wetland.

Another private preserve on the Eastern Shore is the Horsehead Wetlands Center, a five-hundred-acre sanctuary of wetlands, upland, and shallow ponds. The center is operated by the Wildfowl Trust of North America, a nonprofit organization whose mission is to preserve wildfowl and wetlands through education, conservation, and research. The center is just outside of Grasonville near U.S. Route 50.

Eastern Neck Island National Wildlife Refuge is a 2,285-acre preserve whose major constituency is waterfowl. An estimated 40,000 ducks and geese spend the winter on or near the refuge, including great flocks of canvasbacks. Dabbling ducks such as blacks, mallards, and widgeons can be seen in shallows, with diving ducks present in the deeper open waters. Three hiking trails provide access to good birding habitat, and a boat ramp at Bogles Wharf Landing is handy for those who want to explore by water.

Adkins Arboretum in Tuckahoe State Park is a great place to learn about native wetland plants. The arboretum is near Easton and runs along the Tuckahoe River. It encourages visitors to get a close look at native plant species. Indeed, to reach the visitor center, one must park the car and walk across a footbridge that spans a freshwater marsh that hosts dozens of native plants. When the arboretum opened, the marsh was a pond that had been dug years ago, so it was refilled, and a wetland was created. The arboretum also has hiking and biking trails that wind through nearby forests and grasslands.

The best thing about hiking and biking in Maryland is the opportunity to finish the day with a crab cake made of fresh Chesapeake Bay blue crab. Most restaurants have them, and some are excellent and others are disappointing. Crab cakes require a gentle hand, a few spices, and just enough filling to hold the meat together. Done well, a crab cake is tender, juicy, and bursts with the salty sweet flavor of the bay. Bad crab cakes have the flavor and texture of a hockey puck.

You must begin with fresh Chesapeake Bay crabs (not the imported variety). We buy our crabmeat at a small packing plant that employs local women who sit around stainless steel tables and sing spirituals as their fingers fly through hundreds of crabs. The room is filled with the aroma of crabs steaming in a huge vat, and when we pick up our pound of fresh backfin, it is still warm to the touch.

Usually, I'll take the pound of meat home, spoon out a little, mix up some sauce made with ketchup, horseradish, and Old Bay seasoning, and sample the crabmeat before it's time to make crab cakes for dinner. Just checking, you see. Want to make sure that crab is okay before I fix it for the family.

Blackwater Rivers

Eagles gather along the Chesapeake

The fox was crouching in the brown grass, assuming it was well hidden. But the grass wasn't quite tall enough, and we could see it clearly. The fox was a long way from the cornfield and woods and on a sunny day in mid-afternoon was probably feeling a bit exposed. "I seeeee you," I called to the fox.

The fox didn't move a muscle, just crouched there with its head down like a dog in front of a fire. But when a shadow passed over my left shoulder, I could feel the beat of wings, and the fox bolted. A huge bird fell from the sky, dove on the fox, and pulled up just before making contact.

I have seen many bald eagles at a distance, as well as in captivity, but I had never been so close to one in flight, especially when it was hunting. The speed and size of the bird were remarkable; I had no doubt that it could take the fox if it wanted to.

It was a young eagle, probably a third-year bird, according to our *Sibley Guide to Birds.* The tail feathers were mostly white, but still mottled with brown, as was the head. According to Sibley, it's not until the eagle's fourth year that it takes on the striking markings of the adult.

The fox shuffled off to the cornfield with a nonchalant gait, as if it had been smoking in the boys' room and the principal was coming. "Just act natural," it seemed to be saying. The eagle circled and came at the fox again, which by now had almost reached a field of brown standing cornstalks. The eagle made a halfhearted pass, circled again, and disappeared, as did the fox.

This bit of drama unfolded on a Saturday afternoon at Blackwater National Wildlife Refuge on the Eastern Shore of Maryland near the town of Cambridge. Lynn and I go to Blackwater at least once a year, because it's a good place to see waterfowl and in recent years has become the place to go to see bald eagles. Indeed, the eagle that chased the fox was our twelfth of the afternoon. We saw eagles soaring with turkey vultures over the vast marshes, we saw them perched on pine snags, and we saw them resting on exposed tidal flats. The one that chased the fox was memorable.

What makes Blackwater such an eagle magnet? The easy answer is that it has everything an eagle needs: plenty of open space in which to hunt, plentiful food such as fish and small mammals, tall pines to nest in, and an absence of human interference. The area along the Blackwater River south of Cambridge is sparsely populated. It is low country, with farm fields, forests, and vast marshes where muskrats have been trapped for centuries.

When Lynn and I visited, instead of taking the main route (Maryland Route 16) from Cambridge, we turned south in Vienna and made our way along unmarked country roads, crossing wooden, single-lane bridges and driving along causeways that seemed only slightly higher than sea level. We were rewarded with some spectacular scenery, nearly no traffic, and eagle sightings before we got near the refuge.

The Blackwater refuge, at nearly eighteen thousand acres, is vast, and surrounding it are state lands such as Fishing Bay and Taylor's Island Wildlife Management Areas, which add even more to the protected area. So this combination of woodland, open water, farm fields, and wetlands are prime habitat for eagles and many other birds.

The wildlife refuge was created in 1933 to provide wintering grounds for migrating waterfowl, but like most refuges of the era, the constituency has grown in recent years to include a varied list of birds and mammals.

Lynn and I began our tour of Blackwater by stopping at the visitor center to pick up trail maps and look at the interpretive displays, which cover the history and natural history of the Blackwater area. A self-guided wildlife drive begins a short distance past the center, but before getting under way we decided that a walk would give us a chance to stretch our legs and see the refuge up close.

Marsh Edge Trail, near the entrance of Wildlife Drive, is not long, but it covers a remarkable diversity of habitat. We began in a mature loblolly pinewoods, crossed to a transition zone where marsh meets woodland, skirted the open water of Blackwater River, and ended in the pine forest near where we began. It's a great place to see birds other than eagles, herons, and waterfowl. Take things slowly, check the sunlit pine canopy with the binoculars, and you're likely to see nuthatches, chickadees, kinglets, creepers, goldfinches, and a variety of sparrows.

Wildlife Drive runs along an embankment that helped create the freshwater impoundments built for migrating waterfowl. When we visited, there were numerous Canada geese, mallards, pintails, green-winged teal, shovelers, and tundra swans. Great blue herons patrolled the marsh edges, searching for small fish and shellfish.

Blackwater is managed with waterfowl in mind, so the impoundments are planted in seed-producing crops each summer and then flooded in the fall when the ducks begin to arrive. Upland fields are planted with corn and other grains, which are left standing through the winter.

It was in a grassland adjacent to the cornfield that we had our close encounter with the eagle and fox. Refuge officials intended the habitat to benefit visiting waterfowl. A nice bonus is that it also provided a few memorable minutes for a pair of visiting humans.

※ ※ ※

The character of the Chesapeake Bay watershed changes a few miles south of the marshes of Dorchester County. Instead of a landscape of wide, low-lying salt marshes, there are cypress swamps, blackwater rivers, and dense hardwood forests that could be in South Carolina or Georgia rather than in Maryland. The Pocomoke River begins as a trickle in southern Delaware and becomes a major river by the time it empties into the Chesapeake Bay and becomes Pocomoke Sound. The Pocomoke and its major tributary, Nassawango Creek, have been designated by Congress as National Wild and Scenic Rivers. Both are rich in human history and are ecological jewels, with rare plants, birds, and ancient cypress trees that cover the upper parts of the river with a canopy of green. In spring the river and the forests surrounding it are filled with migrating songbirds, most notably the prothonotary warbler, the "swamp canary." The Pocomoke is rewarding to visit during any season, but especially in spring, and especially by canoe.

"See any snakes?" the woman asked. She was loading her gear into a red Old Town canoe and seemed remotely disappointed when we answered in the negative.

My son, Tom, and I eased our canoes into the shallows, exited, and pulled them onto high ground. "No snakes, but lots of birds," I said.

We were on the upper part of the Pocomoke River, where it runs narrow and flat, the color of coffee. The Porter's Crossing bridge spans the river here, and it's a good place to put in and take out. From the bridge, you can see about one hundred feet of river, and then it disappears into a fold of green. Huge cypress trees line the banks of the Pocomoke, their limbs creating a canopy of foliage that makes the river seem dark and mysterious.

This quality of mystery, this darkness, gives the Pocomoke a sinister quality, especially when you stand on a bridge and watch the river disappear into a cypress swamp so huge it could be endless. Our culture has taught us to be wary of swamps. In our literature and our films, swamps are dark places where evil lurks.

But when you enter the Pocomoke by canoe and leave the bridge behind, you will find no evil, only a place of quiet beauty where rare plants grow and where colorful warblers sing in the treetops.

The Pocomoke River begins near the Maryland and Delaware line on the Delmarva Peninsula, where it drains a huge swamp. It winds its way southward down the peninsula, a thin blue line on the map, and doesn't widen appreciably until it nears the town of Snow Hill. From Snow Hill it flows through forest and farmland to Pocomoke City and empties into Pocomoke Sound, which forms the boundary between Maryland and Virginia on the Eastern Shore.

The lower portions of the Pocomoke can be busy, especially on summer weekends as fishermen and recreational boaters take to the water. But if you paddle a canoe, the upper portions of the Pocomoke River and Nassawango Creek can provide a timeless escape from civilization, at least for a day. Much of the forest along the upper river is protected as state forest, or through ownership by the Nature Conservancy, a private land conservation organization.

The town of Snow Hill is a good focal point for exploring the Pocomoke. The community was founded in 1642 and named for a district in London. The river runs through the town, and in years past was key to the commerce of the area, serving as a means of sending valuable timber and iron ore to markets. Today the river is more often a source of recreation. A park and a boat launch facility are on the river, and a few miles south is Shad Landing, a state park where camping and canoe rentals are available.

Pocomoke River Canoe Company is located in an old lumber warehouse on the river, and proprietor Barry Laws offers canoe rentals and a shuttle service to convenient put-ins. If you bring your own boat, you can launch at various locations along the river and either paddle to Snow Hill and get a ride back to your vehicle, or simply paddle out and back. The best put-ins are where bridges cross the river along secondary roadways. Whiton Crossing is about twelve miles north of Snow Hill, and Porter's is about halfway between Whiton and the town. The river here is narrow and winding, although portions between Whiton and Porter's were channelized years ago to improve storm drainage.

A third alternative would be to put in on Nassawango Creek at the bridge on Red House Road. The Nassawango is a tributary of the Pocomoke and joins the river just south of Snow Hill. It's a six-mile paddle from Red House Road to either Snow Hill or Shad Landing.

Canoeing any of these sections of the river will provide a close-up look at a classic cypress swamp. The river is narrow and shallow, and numerous deadfalls make travel by larger boat impractical. So you can paddle all day without encountering motorboats, and on weekdays it's rare even to meet other canoeists.

It's best to approach the Pocomoke slowly, stopping frequently to float with the gentle current and enjoy the sights and sounds of the river. When Tom and I went on our spring trip, the prothonotary warblers were in the middle of mating season, and these bright yellow and gray birds were like jewels in the treetops, especially when one was caught in a shaft of sunlight.

We watched one warbler hopscotching along lily pads as it chased a damselfly. The bird was so busy tracking the insect it ignored us, nearly flying into our canoe.

The river here is flat, but there usually is a current. The water is dark and glossy, metallic almost, and the only time you realize it's moving is when you notice a leaf floating by, or see lily pads slow-dancing in the current.

There are snakes here, but most are harmless water snakes, which, given the alternative, would prefer to have nothing to do with humans. Earlier in the day we had stopped by Pocomoke River Canoe Company and observed a student group in the process of launching. "Watch out for the cottonmouth moccasins," shouted their instructor.

The employee who was assisting the students winced and shook his head. "We're about a hundred miles north of the nearest moccasin," he said. "There are just none here. But people seem to enjoy thinking otherwise."

※ ※ ※

Nassawango Creek is the major tributary of the Pocomoke River, and in early summer the banks are lined with a shrub called fringetree, which has beautiful white flowers. I was wondering whether the aroma might be just as pleasing, so I nudged the canoe into a thicket on the creek shore, grabbed a handful of fringe flowers, and inhaled. It was then that I noticed the snake sprawled across the lower limbs of the shrub.

I looked at the snake, and it looked at me, and neither of us knew quite what to do. I'm not necessarily afraid of snakes, but I don't like being surprised. I'll bet that the snake doesn't either.

And, no, it wasn't a cottonmouth moccasin. It was, as far as I could tell, a northern water snake, but water snakes vary a great deal in color, and this one wasn't wearing a name badge.

Bill Bostian, who was paddling in the stern, slowly edged the canoe out of the thicket, and the snake and I parted company. Bostian works for the Nature Conservancy and he had volunteered to show Lynn and me Nassawango Creek Preserve, which is the largest private nature preserve in the state. The day before our trip, the conservancy had announced a three-year, $67 million campaign to protect natural areas in Maryland and Virginia, and Nassawango was the first major Maryland project of the initiative.

"We basically doubled the size of the preserve," said Bostian. "We purchased 3,520 acres along the Nassawango from the E. S. Adkins Company, making the preserve more than 7,250 acres. The purchase allows us to protect a unique ecosystem along the creek, and it also protects the Chesapeake Bay, because the Nassawango is part of the watershed."

The Nassawango runs for some eighteen miles through the center of the Eastern Shore, joining the Pocomoke River near the town of Snow Hill. I had met Bostian where Red House Road crosses the creek about five miles north of Snow Hill. The conservancy maintains a small canoe launch here, and it makes for a very pleasant float trip to put in at Red House Road and paddle down to Snow Hill.

Bostian describes the Nassawango as a southern cypress swamp, more comparable to habitat found in the southeastern states than the Eastern Shore, where lowlands tend to be grassy and flooded with saltwater. The Nassawango is fresh, even though it is pushed and pulled by the tidal flow of the Chesapeake many miles away.

The water is glossy and black, flowing almost imperceptibly. A few hundred feet from where we put in, the creek takes a left turn and disappears into a fold of cypress and gum. Cypress knees grow out of the shallows on the edge of the creek; huge gums and oaks lean over the water, creating a green canopy that only now and then lets the sun through.

After putting some distance between us and the bridge, we

stopped paddling and listened to the swamp. The number of birds we heard was amazing, even if we could identify only a few of the songs. "We're at the peak of the spring migration," said Bostian. "The swamp is a forested corridor the birds use when they travel, plus we get a lot of birds that nest here, primarily the prothonotary warbler."

We had been seeing prothonotaries since we put in, crossing the creek ahead of us, searching for insects in the tree canopy, or foraging in pickerelweed near the water. It is a spectacular bird with a bright yellow head, breast, and belly, often called the swamp canary for obvious reasons.

As we paddled, we passed giant cypress trees that Bostian said could be more than a century old. "Much of the forest here was cut in the early 1800s, but some of the big trees survived," said Bostian. "An iron furnace was in operation here until 1850, and a lot of the timber was used to make charcoal to fuel the furnace."

Many of us perceive swamps as dark, forbidding places filled with venomous snakes, clouds of biting insects, and various other dangers. The Nassawango, however, was filled with color and not in the least forbidding. Wild azaleas bloomed along the creek shore, the fringetree blossoms were at their height, and birds skittered through the forest canopy like little jewels.

About halfway to Snow Hill is the Fran Uhler Nature Trail, a good spot to stretch the legs, have lunch, and look for wildflowers. The short trail loops from the creek shore to an upland forest, then back through a hardwood swamp to the trailhead. May apple and Solomon's seal were blooming, but a search for lady slippers went unrewarded.

Beyond the nature trail the creek widens and changes character somewhat. The green canopy is replaced by open sky, and the little creek looks more like a proper river.

As we paddled along the shoreline, the sun shone brightly on thickets of fringetree, whose white flowers were drooping in thick clusters. Fringetree, Bostian told me, is also called "old man's beard."

By the way, it has no aroma at all.

Tilghman Island
Rock stars on the twentieth anniversary

When Lynn and I celebrated our twentieth wedding anniversary, we looked for a place to escape to for the weekend. We weren't sure where we wanted to go, but we knew where we *didn't* want to go.

"I don't want to go someplace where they sell Christmas ornaments year round," said Lynn.

"And I don't want to go to a place that has pink, heart-shaped Jacuzzis," I said.

That narrowed it right down.

So we picked a place that offers everything we enjoy: outdoor sports, wonderful food, and friendly and unpretentious service. We went rock fishing at Captain Buddy Harrison's Chesapeake House on Tilghman Island, Maryland.

Truth is, you're not likely to find Tilghman Island on many couples' short list of romantic getaways. Cancun it ain't. This is a working watermen's town, a place where skipjacks still dredge oysters, where boats are used for business as well as pleasure. To reach Tilghman Island you drive to Easton on U.S. Route 50, head west on Maryland Route 33, pass through St. Michaels, and keep driving until the road ends. Welcome to Tilghman Island, where being on the water means work.

And that's why we like Tilghman Island. We like the throaty growl of those diesel-powered deadrises, and we enjoy the dock-side commerce, the unloading of the day's catch of fish, crabs, or oysters. We like to watch those lanky crabhouse cats that belong to no one but instead make up their own community. This is an honest and authentic place, an island that so far has escaped gentrification. It is a place of great beauty.

The Harrison family has operated the Chesapeake House for

more than a century. Back during the days of steamships, Captain Levin Harrison would dock his cargo vessel in Baltimore, and city residents would inquire about places along the bay to escape the summer heat. Captain Harrison's wife, Ida, was a schoolteacher with free time during the summer, and so the family began taking in boarders.

In the early days of the business, the guests were mainly women and children, but later the men began coming with their families, and the Harrisons began taking them fishing.

The fifth generation of the Harrison family is now involved in the business, which is presided over by Captain Levin Harrison III, whom everyone knows simply as Captain Buddy. Captain Buddy has a twinkle in his eye and is quick with a story, and he knows that his family's success in the hospitality business is built upon generations of happy customers. "We do everything we can to please our guests," he says. "We like to see smiling faces."

Like Tilghman Island, Chesapeake House is honest and unpretentious. The main building is a white, two-story frame lodge on the edge of town. The restaurant is attached, and separate guest quarters are located across the lawn. The boat dock is around back.

Guests at Chesapeake House come for two reasons: the food, meaning abundant fresh local seafood; and the fishing, which, depending upon the season, could mean rockfish, bluefish, trout, croakers, flounder, or a mix of the above. A set fee gets you a night's lodging, dinner, breakfast, a fishing trip, and a boxed lunch on the boat.

Dinner is family style and plentiful. On our visit, Captain Buddy was featuring his popular oyster buffet, which presents oysters prepared in nearly every conceivable manner. We began with a plate of raw ones on the half shell, opened for us as we waited. We then sampled creamy oyster stew, single fried oysters, oyster fritters, oysters on the half shell broiled with crab imperial and bacon, and oysters in a Creole sauce with rice. And to add some land-based balance to this seafood feast there was fried chicken, ham, lima beans, stewed tomatoes, and homemade biscuits.

Breakfast is equally ample and is served early. We were on the boat before seven and watched the sunrise aboard the *Lady Peggy* with skipper Allen Bryan as we headed into the Chesapeake to an area called Summer Gooses, which had been a hot spot for rockfish, or striped bass, when we were there.

Captain Allen throttled down the big diesel, turned into the current, and dropped anchor. We would chum and use light spinning rigs, so a sizeable rockfish would be a challenge. I prefer this method to trolling, because you can feel the fish the instant it hits, and the light tackle is more sporting.

Captain Allen used a ladle to spoon out some ground menhaden, which floated off in the current behind us. We then baited up with soft-shell clams and let the baits drift back with the chum. "We're fishing in about thirty feet of water, so we'll put on different size sinkers and fish various depths," said Captain Allen. "Rockfish feed in the entire water column, so we'll do some experimenting."

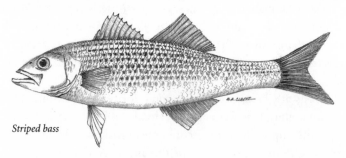

Striped bass

The idea is for the chum to attract the fish, which then will take your bait. For the first fifteen minutes or so, the menhaden attracted only gulls, and then Lynn's rod dipped, the drag began singing, and we had engaged our first rockfish of the day.

Captain Allen leaned over the stern, netted the fish, and measured it. It was a tad under eighteen inches, the legal minimum, and so we gently released it.

But by lunchtime there would be more than two dozen others, some keepers and some not. Lynn caught one just before quitting time that measured more than twenty-three inches, and that one came home with us. On the following evening, her catch, glazed with rosemary butter, graced our dinner table.

❈ ❈ ❈

It was just before dawn and the *City of Norfolk* was steaming into the port of Baltimore. The sky was cool magenta and the state-room lights looked warm and inviting. They reflected in the calm water of the harbor, flickering like dozens of small fires.

The date was July 5, 1961, and this stately Old Bay Line steamboat was making one of her last runs, ferrying passengers and assorted goods up and down the Chesapeake Bay. In a little over a year she would be gone, and her passing would mark the end of an era, an irreversible change in the way people in tidewater moved people and things.

The *City of Norfolk* last sailed to Baltimore more than forty years ago, but her spirit lives on in the Chesapeake Bay Maritime Museum on the Miles River in the town of St. Michaels. St. Michaels once was a leathery little community of shipbuilders and watermen, but now is described in travel literature as "quaint and charming," which usually means there are lots of shops that sell hundred-dollar golf shirts.

But St. Michaels actually is a pleasant place to visit, friendly and unassuming, even though there is at least one shop where you can decorate your Christmas tree in August. You pass through St. Michaels on the way to and from Tilghman Island, so Lynn and I stopped to have lunch and visit the maritime museum on our way home from the rockfishing trip. We had lunch in a little restaurant on Talbot Street, and the waitress treated us like we were visiting family. Lynn had cream of crab soup, and the waitress volunteered to bring her a bit of sherry to flavor it. She returned shortly to report that someone had pilfered both decanters she had stashed in the kitchen, and her tone of voice indicated she had a suspect in mind. She left the restaurant and walked down the street to borrow sherry from a neighbor.

The Chesapeake Bay Maritime Museum contradicts the usual

perception of what a museum should be. This is not a place of dusty artifacts lodged in a shadowy building with uniformed guards. Indeed, most of our time at the museum was spent outdoors, walking.

The museum more closely resembles a campus than an archive. It is spread over eighteen acres of waterfront, with many restored buildings, boat warehouses, shops, and galleries. An 1879 lighthouse, which once stood at Hooper Strait, is a focal point of the museum grounds. The bandstand that once echoed with Glenn Miller tunes at Tolchester Beach is nearby. Other buildings explore the role the bay has played in American history, in the waterfowl hunting tradition of the Chesapeake, and in the economic ebb and flow of Chesapeake Bay communities and families.

This is an active museum, where in warmer weather you can watch watermen sort their catch, take sailing lessons, or learn to build your own boat or carve a hunting decoy. Restoration is an ongoing process at St. Michaels. Historic buildings are being restored, and a large shed houses old boats in various stages of repair. Visitors are encouraged to watch and ask questions.

The Steamboat Building is one of the largest on the grounds. It explores the role mechanical power played in shaping the lives of those who worked and played on the bay, and there are many artifacts from the steam era, including the dramatic photograph of the *City of Norfolk* making her way into Baltimore Harbor in 1961.

The maritime museum is rapidly growing, and it seems that each time we visit there is a new addition. This time it was a building devoted to oystering on the Chesapeake. The building encloses a life-size Chesapeake Bay skipjack, a sailing craft used to dredge oysters on the bay. Various displays explain the role of the oyster in the economy and ecology of the Chesapeake Bay region.

When Lynn and I visited in early fall, the leaves on the hardwood trees were beginning to turn various shades of red and gold. Driving to St. Michaels was like taking a cruise through a greeting card scene. This is farm country, laced by meandering rivers and streams. In gently rolling fields, bent and weathered stalks of corn stood against the fall sky. In most fields, flocks of Canada geese were bent over, feeding, while a lone sentinel kept a lookout. On the horizon, more geese were trading back and forth between fields, flying in ragged strings.

On our way home we decided to get off the highway, take to the back roads, and explore the countryside. Outside of the city of Salisbury, at the community of White Haven, you cross the Wicomico River by taking a little three-car ferry that moves along on a steel cable. It's one of the few small ferries in the east that has not yet been replaced by a bridge. After a day at the maritime museum, it seemed a fitting way to return home.

Tylerton

A little silent music please, maestro

I *think what I'll do is go down to the filling station and get me a bottle of soda pop. Yep, I'm going to go down to the filling station and get me a bottle of soda pop, and then I'm going to go over to Thelma Lou's and watch a little teevee.*

I was sitting on the front porch watching the sun sparkle on Tyler Creek, and I was feeling a lot like Barney Fife after Sunday dinner, sitting on Andy and Aunt Bee's porch, Andy strumming the guitar, humming "Just as I Am," Aunt Bee gently rocking. It was August and warm outside, but the porch was shady. A ceiling fan spun overhead, slightly off balance, a blade tap-tapping but still creating a white hum and a cool breeze. An urn filled with ice water was on the table next to my chair. It was sweating and had created a puddle. I realized I should clean it up, and would do so eventually.

One does not make haste in Tylerton. Tylerton is on Smith Island in the Chesapeake Bay, a boat ride of about forty-five minutes from Crisfield. Visiting here is like stepping back in time, or having time suspended. There are no cars on Tylerton, because none are needed. There is no place to go. Narrow streets thread their way through the community, and now and then a bicycle and rider will pass, perhaps a golf cart driven by someone bringing home groceries. The streets end either at the edge of the creek or in someone's backyard.

On first visiting Tylerton, the initial urge is to do something, explore the place, meet some people. And so I walked the streets of Tylerton twice, and then covered them once by bicycle. I saw the church, the tiny post office, the co-op where the women of Tylerton pick crabs and pack crabmeat for market, and then I had a wonderful crab cake sandwich at the Drum Point Market, Tylerton's only store. And I was only two hours into a three-day visit.

It takes at least two hours to leave behind the mainland frame of mind and get yourself on Tylerton time. Lynn and I had booked a room at the Inn of Silent Music, an appropriately named bed-and-breakfast that's on the south end of the community, overlooking Tyler Creek, Sassafras Hammock, and the Virginia state line. In the distance, to the south, is the island of Tangier. Across Tyler Creek are the two other Smith Island communities, Rhodes Point and Ewell. Both are larger than Tylerton, which has a population of about seventy, and both are connected by roads and have cars.

We arrived at Tylerton aboard the *Captain Jason II,* a diesel-powered passenger ferry that crosses Tangier Sound twice daily, carrying people and produce. On most trips, freshly packed crab-meat and soft-shell crabs move from Tylerton to Crisfield. On the return trip, mainland staples such as butter, eggs, and fresh fruit make their way to Tylerton. It is a very pleasurable way to go about commerce.

Most of the butter, eggs, and fresh fruit are headed either to Drum Point Market or to the Inn of Silent Music, Tylerton's two major commercial ventures. The inn is owned and operated by LeRoy Friesen and his wife, Sharryl Lindberg, both of whom retreated to Tylerton in 1997 when they were in their early fifties. LeRoy was a Mennonite who converted to Roman Catholicism and today is very active in the small congregation of Tylerton's United Methodist Church. Sharryl taught children's literature in a university, and LeRoy taught theology in a seminary. They later worked in the hospitality industry in Washington, D.C.

LeRoy and Sharryl are Tylerton's only two full-time "foreigners," as non-native islanders are known. They discovered the community on a vacation trip, bought a rather weathered two-story frame home in 1995, and opened the Inn of Silent Music in May 1997. The name seems a bit curious to first-time visitors, but once you've been in Tylerton for a while, you begin to catch on. "Over the years, the notion of 'silent music' has caught my attention in the work of several different writers," says LeRoy. "St. John of the Cross wrote a poem called 'The Spiritual Canticle' that includes the lines 'the tranquil night / at the time of the rising dawn / silent music / sounding solitude / the supper that refreshes, and deepens love.'"

The concept of silent music and sounding solitude, says LeRoy, refers to a spiritual harmony, a music so sublime it surpasses all concerts and melodies of the world. The music is silent because it brings tranquil and quiet knowledge without the need for the sound of voices.

"In 1994 Sharryl and I rented a cottage north of what is now the inn, and we spent our vacation on the porch, reading, observing wildlife, and never missing a sunset over Rhodes Point," says LeRoy. "As the weeks passed we realized that the natural environment was having a marked impact on us, slowing down our urban rhythms, initiating us into silence, generating within us the harmony played out around us, and eliciting awe and gratitude and joy. In short, like many other natural settings, this one seemed to be spiritually evocative. It impacted our internal and relational landscapes. So when we envisioned opening the inn, we wanted our guests to have some of the same experiences we had, and we wanted the name of the inn to hint at such a vision."

LeRoy Friesen is a tall, sturdily built Minnesotan who in August favors T-shirts, Bermuda shorts, and a white apron. His thick, graying blond hair is held in place by a yellow headband. Like another well-known Minnesotan, the humorist Garrison Keillor, LeRoy enjoys telling a good story and often will entertain dinner guests with tales of the history and people of Smith Island. LeRoy meets arrivals at the Tylerton boat dock with a garden cart, loads their luggage, and gives them a tour of the community on the walk back to the inn.

While LeRoy entertains the guests and gets them settled into their rooms, Sharryl spends her time in the kitchen, turning out breakfasts that might include coffee, fresh fruit, an artichoke frittata, and hot bread. Dinners usually are centered on local seafood:

crabmeat, fried soft crabs, or broiled rockfish caught earlier in the day by guests. Sharryl is tall and thin and wears her hair cropped short. Like LeRoy, she has a background in academics. The numerous bookcases in the inn are filled to overflowing, with everything from books on art and spirituality to suspense novels.

"We were married in 1990 and both of us were teaching, I at a seminary and Sharryl at a university, and the outlook for us getting jobs at the same school was not good," says LeRoy. "So we decided to throw it wide open. We wanted to work together, and we wanted work that was meaningful. So we left the university setting and took a position in the hospitality industry, with the Quakers in DuPont Circle in Washington."

LeRoy and Sharryl stayed with the Quakers for nearly eight years, entertaining international guests at their headquarters in the capital. After purchasing the home that would become the inn in 1995, they spent the next thirty months commuting between Washington and Tylerton, slowly renovating and expanding the building, bringing furniture from the mainland on the small ferry one piece at a time. They had their first guests on Memorial Day weekend in 1997 and had a busy summer as word of the inn spread. In 1998 they doubled their occupancy rate, and in 1999 doubled it again. Through the summer season their three guest rooms are usually filled on weekends and on about 75 percent of weeknights as well.

It seems an odd mix, this isolated fishing village and a pair of academics who would seem more at home in an urban university environment where museums and libraries are easily at hand. But LeRoy and Sharryl have thrived here, and they discovered that they have more in common with their Tylerton neighbors than one might first believe. Most important, they share deep spiritual beliefs with the people of the community. It's true that their religious background is more liberal and academic than the conservative beliefs of the United Methodists, but the feeling of spirituality is real, and it is shared.

It takes a great deal of religious faith to live on an island. There must be trust that the tide will rise only so far, and then ebb. The certainty of the tides, the faith in rise and fall, is the cornerstone of life. Although the village is only a few feet above sea level, the residents have faith that their spiritual beliefs will keep them safe. If they pray hard enough, the storms will pass them by.

The adjustment from life in the city to life on an island was made gradually, and that helped. "We commuted for two and a half years," says Sharryl. "We would be here for a long weekend, working on the house, and on Sunday we would go back to Washington. So we had that to fall back on. Our concern, when we opened the inn, was what our feeling would be when Sunday came and there was no place to go back to."

The answer to that question was provided by the inn itself. "It's true that Tylerton is very different than Washington, but our daily life isn't that different," says Sharryl. "We have our guests, most of whom come from the city, and running the inn is a full-time job for both of us. We are immersed in it. We didn't have the time to reflect and wonder what we'd be doing if we were in Washington. This has become home, and we're happy here."

In visiting Tylerton and Smith Island, one comes away with the impression of great natural beauty and solitude, yet there is a feeling that borders on sadness, a suspicion that we may be witnessing life in the Chesapeake Bay as it may never be again. In Tylerton all the men work on the water; the women find work in the cooperative, picking crabs and packing crabmeat for market. The economic blood of the island is the Chesapeake and the fish and shellfish it produces. To a large extent, that means blue crabs. Oysters, which once were plentiful and provided jobs and income in winter, are now scarce. It is difficult to make a living working on the water, and the young people are leaving. Neighboring communities such as Tangier and Ewell have embraced tourism and the dollars it brings, but Tylerton steadfastly remains a community of working watermen.

"We have some young men here who would like to stay and work on the water, but they can make more money on the mainland," says Sharryl. "And if they want to marry and have a family, it's difficult to find a young woman who is willing to adapt to island life. If they want to work, the only opportunity here is the co-op, picking crabs."

And so the population of Tylerton has gotten smaller, and older. Many of the homes are now owned by seasonal residents, who spend most of the year on the mainland. The economy is boosted somewhat by the inn, which employs a part-time neighbor. Visitors are urged to use the services of local guides for sightseeing and fishing trips, and the inn attempts to purchase at least half of its kitchen supplies from Drum Point Market. Still, the word LeRoy uses in describing life here is "endangered." The young people are leaving, and the sea is rising. "The reality is that the island is sinking and the sea level is slowly rising," says LeRoy. "The Corps of Engineers built a bulkhead on the west side of the village in 2002, and it has helped. But it's only a temporary fix."

※ ※ ※

Waverly Evans's blond hair has been bleached by the sun and by the years. He is seventy-eight and still runs a line of crab pots, still scrapes hard crabs in the shallow creeks that thread through the marshes of Smith Island. He was born in the settlement of Long Branch, one of several little communities that dotted the upland ridges of Smith Island. We cruised by Long Branch in Waverly's twenty-foot center-console skiff. He lit a cigarette and took a deep drag. "That's where I grew up," he says. "I lived there until I was nine or ten years old. There were ten homes there then."

Today there are a few stunted pines and cedars, some saltwater bush. Long Branch is just another hammock, a slight rise in the marsh where a few upland shrubs grow. Waverly's house was loaded onto a barge and moved to Tylerton shortly after a hurricane devastated the coast in August 1933. It still stands in the northern part of the community, not far from his dock and the shanty where he sheds soft crabs and packs them for market.

Waverly goes crabbing in the morning and in the afternoon takes visitors out fishing or to look for birds in nearby Martin National Wildlife Refuge. "These marshes are full of birds," he says. "We've got storks, white cranes, all kinds of birds."

He laughs at himself. "My wife tells me if I'm going to take people out to look for birds, I've got to get one of those guidebooks that identifies them."

Waverly might not know his birds, but he definitely knows where to find them. We turned into a shallow creek in the wildlife refuge, passed a thick stand of pines called Joe's Ridge, and found the treetops filled with herons, a huge rookery that covered acres of isolated woodland. There were snowy egrets, great blue herons, tricolored and little blue herons, green herons, yellow-crowned and black-crowned night herons. Nearby were dozens of ospreys, a bald eagle, and a pair of peregrine falcons that had been using a hacking tower constructed for them. Black ducks, their silver underwings shining in the sun, flushed in pairs from marsh ponds.

Waverly's outboard was pumping sand. He nudged the trim switch and tilted the propeller upward. Still, a plume of sand followed in our wake. We were in shallow water that years ago might have been upland or high marsh. If you look at old charts of Smith Island, they show a lot more green, or upland. Today, the predominant color is blue. You once could walk all the way from Kedges Straits down the length of Smith Island, through Rhodes Point, down Hog Neck to Shanks Island and Goose Island, all the way to Tangier. Much of the area is now covered by water.

"When I was growing up there were farms here, people grew vegetables and had cattle, hogs, and chickens," says Waverly. "There were cattle all over these marshes and you had to be careful if you got out and walked on the marsh. There's a story about a fellow who lived on Goat Island who had a pretty young daughter, and a young man from Ewell wanted to go visit her. So he sailed up to Goat Island, beached his boat, and started walking. Pretty soon he meets this big bull right in the middle of the path, so he turned around and came right back home. 'What happened to you?' his friends asked. 'Well,' he said, 'It was either the bull or the bay, and I took the bay.' People here still use that phrase when they're faced with a conflict—'It's either the bull or the bay.'"

Assateague Island

Miles of beach and water stretched thin

I was standing in the middle of Baltimore Boulevard, watching a pair of deer as they watched me. The larger of the two nibbled on the other's ear, and then he ran off into a pine thicket. The other deer soon followed.

Baltimore Boulevard does not get a lot of traffic these days. What remains of it runs like a series of asphalt dashes down the spine of Assateague Island. There will be a dune, a heather bald, and then a black dash about two feet higher than the surrounding sand. In the late 1950s developers were planning a massive residential and recreational resort here, something to rival Ocean City, which lies on the next island north, just across the inlet. They ferried potential investors across Sinepuxent Bay, docked on the western side of the island, and then drove them fifteen miles down Baltimore Boulevard south to the Virginia line. Nine thousand building lots were laid out, and land was cleared for 130 side streets intersecting Baltimore Boulevard.

But in March 1962 a vicious northeast storm struck the East Coast, flooding Assateague and other barrier islands, doing millions of dollars worth of damage. The Ash Wednesday storm, as it became known, destroyed most of Baltimore Boulevard, and with it the plans for an extensive resort development on Assateague. After witnessing the destruction brought about by the storm, potential buyers looked elsewhere for vacation homes. Three years later Assateague became a national seashore, and these thick streaks of asphalt are all that remain of the potential resort. Gulls put them to good use, catching clams in Sinepuxent Bay and dropping them on the hard surface to break them.

On a calm summer afternoon, with the sun baking the dunes, it's difficult to imagine what it might have been like here on that day in March 1962. The storm was so violent the scars still remain many years later. In a maritime forest nearby there is a small freshwater pool about eight feet deep. It's not a natural spring. The pool was created when the ocean picked up a house and its foundation, carried it to the spot, and then whirled around it long enough to scour out the deep pool. The house was later burned to water level, but parts of the foundation still remain on the bottom of the pool. After witnessing such a thing, I would be hesitant to build a house on Assateague.

Assateague is a large island, more than thirty miles long, with the southern portion in Virginia and the northern part in Maryland. Assateague Island State Park is on the northern end of the island, and the national seashore begins a bit farther south. The Virginia portion of the island includes Chincoteague National Wildlife Refuge.

While the Virginia portion of Assateague is accessed via the town of Chincoteague, to reach the Maryland end you take U.S. Route 113 to the town of Berlin, Maryland, turn right on state Route 376, right again on state Route 611, and make your way across Verrazano Bridge to the island. Assateague here is low and

Ponies on Assateague Island

narrow, with a few loblolly pine forests among the bayberry thickets and tidal marshes. The vulnerability of the island to storms is
apparent from atop the bridge. It is a slender finger of sand, a tenuous bit of land separating Sinepuxent Bay from the Atlantic.
Look north and there's the skyline of Ocean City, an unlikely oasis
that seems to hover over the ocean.

Baltimore Boulevard has been reduced to asphalt scrap, but it
has been replaced by Bayberry Drive, which runs from the bridge
and state park southward for some four miles, with a paved bike
path alongside. Although Assateague did not become a second
Ocean City, its ocean beach makes it a popular summer destination, often luring vacationing families who want to escape the
traffic and crowds of nearby Ocean City for a day.

But Assateague offers more than just a beach. The national
seashore has three interpretive hiking trails that feature the different natural communities of the island. Turn right on Bayside Drive
just past the national seashore entrance and Life of the Marsh Trail
will be on the left. It's a loop of about one-half mile and offers a
good view of Sinepuxent Bay and the salt marsh that makes up the
bayside margin of the island.

Farther along Bayberry Drive is Life of the Forest Trail, another
half-mile loop that takes you through a loblolly pine forest,
through thickets of greenbrier and phragmites, and then along a
transition zone where upland meets salt marsh. The wooded area
is a great place to see songbirds such as warblers and thrushes during the spring migration.

Life of the Dunes Trail begins and ends at the cul-de-sac at the
end of Bayberry Drive. Here you can learn how dunes are sculpted
by wind, water, and other forces, and you can see an extensive
variety of dune plants, such as American beachgrass and beach
heather. The asphalt dashes, the remains of Baltimore Boulevard,
are along this trail.

If you have camping on your mind, you have several choices.
Bayside sites are available across the road from Life of the Marsh
Trail. Most are in a wooded area and include picnic tables and
charcoal grills. Closer to the beach, camping areas are provided

behind the primary dune line along Bayberry Drive. These are primitive sites, with few amenities. If you want to get away from the crowds, several walk-in campsites are available farther south, and canoe-in sites are situated along the bayside.

Keep in mind that this is camping in the rough. When the weather warms, insects can be bothersome, and in hot weather there is little shade to provide relief. If the wind is blowing, it's nearly impossible to keep sand out of your tent and sleeping bag, and if it's really blowing, you could find that your tent has transformed itself into a kite.

Ah, but it's worth it. Hike those trails, walk that beach, enjoy that gourmet dinner of sand-infused macaroni and cheese, and then turn in for the night. Hear that? It's the rhythm of the surf. It's wild and ancient, and it reminds us how huge this world is and how vulnerable and fragile we are. And that's something to sleep on.

※ ※ ※

I hunt. I gather. The bayside of Assateague Island is a great place to go clamming. As an old waterman once told me, "Son, there's a lot of water out there, but it's stretched mighty thin."

I drove across Verrazano Bridge toward Assateague, looked to the south, and people were standing in the middle of Sinepuxent Bay. They weren't in boats, weren't swimming, but were standing there on the bottom, in waist-deep water. Talk about stretched thin.

I parked the car at the old ferry dock, where a volunteer naturalist was giving lessons in the fine art of catching a clam. He had a plastic bucket with a swimming pool float called a "noodle" wrapped around it. A string was attached to the bucket, and he tied the string to his waist and the floating bucket followed along behind him as he slowly walked through the shallow water searching for clams. I looked into his bucket and saw that he already had more than a dozen clams, ranging in size from small littlenecks, about an inch and a half in diameter, to large chowder clams, which were three or four inches.

He was catching clams with a rake, pulling it along slowly across the firm bottom. Now and then the tines would scrape across the shell of a clam, and he would dig it out, rinse the sand off, and deposit it in his bucket. As I watched, more and more clammers began to arrive, most carrying new rakes with varnished handles and clean metal parts. It wouldn't take the sand long to dull those handles, and the saltwater would soon put a nice patina of rust on the metal.

Clamming is a traditional sport of the coast, a very enjoyable way of earning your dinner, and it was good to see all of those tourists trying their hand at it. I wished them well. Most had probably never eaten clams they had caught themselves, and I knew the successful clammers would be in for a pleasant surprise. Wild hard-shell clams, *Mercenaria mercenaria,* taste nothing at all like clams you buy in a grocery store. Commercial clam strips are tough and flavorless. And Americans have been led to believe there are only two choices in chowder: Manhattan, which is red, and New England, which is creamy. A pox on the soup companies for fostering such rubbish. Let me tell you a little about clams.

I learned to clam by going out with my father and his friends. We would anchor the boat in a shallow bay, grab a clam rake, and begin scraping the bottom. When the tines struck a clam, I would pry it out, rinse it off, and place it in a bushel basket I had wedged inside a tire tube. If we had located good clamming ground, I would fill the basket in an hour or so. That evening, there would be clam fritters for dinner, served with boiled potatoes and fresh butterbeans and corn on the cob. Some clams would go into the freezer, and when the weather turned chilly in the fall, my mother would make clam chowder, rich with fresh potatoes and bacon. If we caught small clams, called littlenecks or cherrystones, we would steam them open and have them with melted butter. Sweet, salty, tender steamed clams. *Mercenaria* at its best.

The wonderful thing about clamming is that you don't have to spend a lot of money to enjoy the sport. You will find no titanium-shafted clamming rakes in the pages of L. L. Bean. Your sporting goods retailer will not have expensive Nike clamming shoes. There are no clamming magazines to subscribe to, no nonprofit organizations whose noble goal it is to save the clam, and in most states you will not even have to write a check to the government for the privilege of gathering a few clams. Nor should you worry about the proper clamming wardrobe. Fashionable clamming attire usually resembles thrift shop discards.

There are basically three ways to catch clams: *raking*, as we did in the shallow waters of Sinepuxent Bay; *signing*, or looking for evidence of a clam's presence on an exposed tidal flat; and *treading*, which means simply walking along the soft bottom until you feel the stonelike presence of a clam beneath your foot.

The only tools you'll need are something to pry the clam from the bottom and a basket to store your catch. When clams are found in a soft bottom, they can usually be freed with the toes. Through the process of evolution, humans have become very ineffective at using the lower digits. Seasoned clammers, however, are second only to the primates in lower digital dexterity. A good clammer can

Clams

pry that clam loose with the toes, scoot it over to the other leg, and use the toes to lift it up the leg until the hands can reach it.

Until you develop such ability, you will need a clam rake or pick to pry the clam loose and bring it to the basket. Rakes and picks are available in most outdoor shops in coastal communities. A garden rake could be used in a pinch, but a clam rake has longer tines, which make it easier to find clams, and they give you more leverage when prying the clam from the tidal flat. If you must select a clamming tool from the garden section, try a hand cultivator. These have three or four tines of the proper length, although the tool lacks the width of the rake.

A clam pick is a smaller version of the rake. A pick usually has two tines, and most have short handles. These were obviously designed by people who were either extremely short or who have never actually been clamming. I have a clam pick made by a local waterman. It has the usual two-tine terminal hardware, but the handle is nearly four feet long, meaning that I don't have to bend over when I want to investigate whether that keyhole-shape opening in the flat is actually the sign of a clam.

Raking clams is hard work, and my preferred method of gathering clams is signing, or looking for evidence of a clam on a flat exposed at low tide. Clams hide an inch or so beneath the surface of the bottom, and they extend two siphons upward, one to pull in water and nutrients, the other to expel waste. If you can find where these siphons broke the surface of the bottom, you can usually find the clam. What we are looking for is clam sign, the telltale holes left in the flat by the siphons, or a bit of clam scat, or perhaps the splatter of water around a hole left when the clam last pumped out. Once the clam sign has been spotted, the pick is used first to confirm the presence of the clam, and then to pry it free of the flat.

But there are times when, for whatever reason, clams do not make sign. Perhaps they have not been eating or pumping out waste, or perhaps the scent of a predator caused them to burrow deep beneath the surface. At times like these, the rake is your best friend, especially if you really need some hot clam chowder. Also, some of the best clamming areas are those covered by water at all tides, meaning you can't see the sign even if it is there. So the rake is your best tool in this situation also.

A third method of clamming is called wading, or treading. You simply wade in shallow water where the bottom is fairly soft and muddy, and you feel the clams with your feet. It's best not to do this barefooted, because there are sharp oyster shells and other dangerous objects lurking about. Old sneakers work, but if the soles are thick it is difficult to feel the clams. Water shoes work better and are lighter in weight—besides, they are designed to get wet. Local watermen here on the coast used to make flannel slippers to wear when treading clams. The flannel gave their feet a measure of protection, and it allowed them to take advantage of the natural dexterity of the toes so that they could free the clam and lift it at least high enough to reach with the hands.

Whether raking, signing, or treading, you will need something to put your clams in. A heavy-duty plastic basket or bucket will do, but most hardware stores in coastal communities have baskets made of galvanized steel designed specifically for clamming. These will not soon rust or corrode, are impervious to sunlight (unlike plastic), and are constructed in a wire-mesh fashion so you can wash the mud off your clams by sloshing them around in seawater.

When my father taught me to clam, we used an old wooden bushel basket suspended in a tire tube. If we were treading clams, or raking in shallow water, we would tie the basket and tube to our waist and pull it along with us as we clammed. The method worked perfectly for some time, but wooden baskets do not take kindly to regular immersions in saltwater, and one day, when being lifted from water to boat, the basket bottom broke free, spilling its contents of one hundred or so hard-won clams back from whence they came. It was then that my father recognized the advantages of investing in professional-level clamming equipment, such as galvanized metal baskets.

VIRGINIA

A Coastal Wilderness

THERE ARE FEW PLACES LEFT IN AMERICA WHERE YOU CAN walk for miles on an ocean beach and not see another soul, not see a roadway, a house, or some other contrivance of humans. There are few places left where you can paddle a canoe for a day and have the waterway to yourself. There are few places left where you can look across miles of salt meadow and not see houses and power poles in the distance. On the coast of Virginia's Eastern Shore is the last of our coastal wilderness, seventy-odd miles of barrier island beaches, salt marsh, and shallow bays that are pretty much the way the Europeans found them when they settled here in the early 1600s.

I think it's important to have places like this, and it's not simply a matter of preserving a relic, of protecting a landscape and saying "this is what a barrier island ecosystem looked like before the resort was constructed, before the dunes were built by bulldozers, before the highway came through, before the bridge was built to the mainland." I think it's good that we can protect some final vestiges of American wilderness, whether it's a mountain range in California, a desert in Utah, or a chain of barrier islands on the Virginia coast. We have too few places where we can go and not see evidence of human manipulation.

And I know I'm in the minority. Wilderness is like a vacuum, a space that must be filled, a blank page begging for the scribbling of humans. Instead of looking at this seventy-mile chain of islands as a special place, a unique landscape, most of us can't resist the urge to find something to do with it, to make it of use to humans. In 1955 the U.S. Navy thought the largest of the islands would make a good target for its bombers. They wanted to bulldoze the maritime forest, create target areas, and have their pilots do some prac-

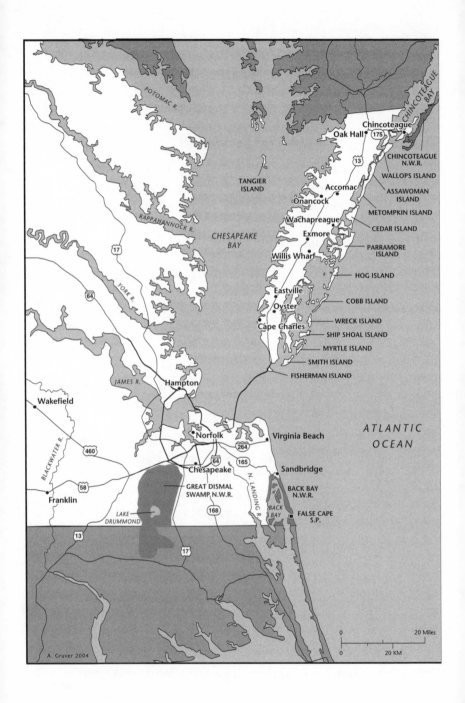

POTOMAC R.

CHINCOTEAGUE BAY

Chincoteague

Oak Hall • (175)

(13)

CHINCOTEAGUE
N.W.R.

WALLOPS ISLAND

ASSAWOMAN
ISLAND

METOMPKIN ISLAND

CEDAR ISLAND

Accomac

TANGIER
ISLAND

Onancock

RAPPAHANNOCK R.

Wachapreague

Exmore

CHESAPEAKE
BAY

Willis Wharf

PARRAMORE
ISLAND

HOG ISLAND

Eastville

COBB ISLAND

Oyster

17

YORK R.

64

WRECK ISLAND

Cape Charles

SHIP SHOAL ISLAND

MYRTLE ISLAND

SMITH ISLAND

FISHERMAN ISLAND

JAMES R.

Hampton

Wakefield

ATLANTIC
OCEAN

Norfolk

Virginia Beach

64

264

BLACKWATER R.

460

Chesapeake

165

Sandbridge

58

GREAT DISMAL
SWAMP N.W.R.

N. LANDING R.

BACK BAY
N.W.R.

Franklin

168

LAKE
DRUMMOND

BACK
BAY

FALSE CAPE
S.P.

13

17

0   20 Miles

0   20 KM

A. Gruver 2004

tice bombing. Local businesspeople worried that the bombing would ruin the sport fishing industry and destroy valuable oyster rocks, and residents of nearby mainland towns fretted over what might happen should a young pilot release his ordnance a mite shy of the target. Eventually, the navy dropped the proposal.

The islands later became the target of resort developers, and when the Nature Conservancy began buying islands in the early 1970s to protect them from development, local opinion was overwhelmingly negative. Some saw conservancy ownership as a lost opportunity for profit; others worried that the islands would wash away unless protected and improved. "Some wondered how the conservationists would protect the island from destruction by the sea. Apparently the answer is that they have no intention to attempt such a thing," wrote the *Eastern Shore News* in 1970.

Today the Virginia barrier islands are the only chain in the mid-Atlantic that retains its geological purity. The berm, the dunes, the forests, and the salt marsh are sculpted by the vagaries of weather. Sand builds up in some areas, it wears away in others. An inlet closes, another one opens. The islands move in response to the sea; they have not yet been destroyed by it.

There are few natural beaches left in the mid-Atlantic. Even in wildlife refuges and national seashores, the dune line is likely to have been built by bulldozers rather than by natural forces. On a recent visit to Assateague Island we found the primary dune to be unnaturally steep and tall, a barricade that stretched for miles separating the ocean from the parking area and roadway behind it. The next northeast storm will easily breech it, despite the sand fencing and the neat rows of beach grass planted on it.

And so it puzzles me that so few people find value in islands as a wilderness landscape, a place of great natural beauty, where one can go for a day and escape the sometimes stifling nearness of civilization. I can understand developers coveting the islands as a potential profit source, but I can't understand how others can be blind to the landscape, to the point of defacing it. At this writing, a proposal is on the table to build a "wind farm" just offshore of the southernmost islands. The proposal calls for the construction of 150 windmills 400 feet high in the ocean off the beach. The *Virginian-Pilot* newspaper in Norfolk, in a lead editorial, praised the plan, arguing that even though it would threaten wildlife and mar the landscape, it didn't matter, because no one lives on the islands. "The view isn't an issue," the newspaper concluded.

I can perhaps sympathize with editorial writers who have spent too much time on Brambleton Avenue in downtown Norfolk. They need to get out in a boat, walk a beach that doesn't have a boardwalk and T-shirt stands, and walk among dunes that were not created by heavy equipment. I am all for finding alternatives to fossil fuel, but you don't destroy the last of our coastal wilderness to do it. Put the windmills off Virginia Beach, paint mermaids on the blades, and shine spotlights on them at night. They'll do double duty as tourist attractions.

The Last of
the Silence

Seventy miles of unspoiled barrier beach

Along Virginia's Eastern Shore lie eighteen barrier islands that are the last of our coastal wilderness on the mid-Atlantic. The islands stretch for some seventy miles, from Assateague on the north to Fisherman Island at the tip of the Eastern Shore peninsula. For the most part, the islands are wild and natural, much as they were when the Europeans settled here in the early 1600s. Wallops Island is the site of a NASA launch facility, and Assateague is home to Chincoteague National Wildlife Refuge and Assateague National Seashore, but the sixteen other islands are remote and relatively untouched by the human hand.

They are what remains of the wilderness that once lined the East Coast of the United States. On these islands you can walk for hours and see only gulls and shorebirds, sand dunes and breaking surf, and endless ocean. The island system is large enough, and remote enough, to be considered a true coastal wilderness, providing the same gifts to humans as do the mountain ranges and canyonlands of the West, even if these islands are somewhat more hemmed in by civilization.

The important thing about wilderness, any wilderness, is the effect it has on the human spirit. Hiking a wilderness beach is different than hiking a resort beach, or even a national seashore beach, where development is held to a minimum. It has to do, I think, with the great value of seclusion, with places that are wild and remote and that provide the illusion, if only for a few hours or a few days, of being untouched. A wilderness beach is defiled by a modest two-lane highway because it destroys the illusion of remoteness. A single house on a remote island or on a salt marsh defiles it for similar reasons.

We need barrier island wildernesses for the same reasons we need wildernesses in the mountains, canyons, or deserts of the southwest. In the words of writer, professor, and environmentalist Wallace Stegner, "Wilderness . . . has helped form our character and . . . has certainly shaped our history as a people. . . . Something will have gone out of us as a people of we ever let the remaining wilderness be destroyed; if we permit the last virgin forests to be turned into comic books and plastic cigarette cases . . . and push our paved roads through the last of the silence, so that never again will Americans be free in their own country from the noise, the exhausts, the stinks of human and automotive waste" (in The *Sound of Mountain Water;* Garden City, NY: Doubleday, 1969).

When it comes to America's coast, precious little silence remains; we have pushed our paved roads through the best of it. Saving wilderness, after all, is an undemocratic process, one that runs counter to our tradition of equal rights, equal access, and the sovereignty of private property.

The very concept of wilderness is unfair because it is exclusionary and elitist. But to democratize wilderness is to eliminate it. The roads, bridges, causeways, parking lots, restrooms, bathhouses, nature centers, and interpretive trails that ensure equal access to all are the very elements that destroy wilderness. By making wilderness accessible—by democratizing it—we transform it into a caricature of itself. It no longer is the real thing, but becomes instead a model, a life-size diorama, complete with video programs and interpretive booklets to explain to us what we are looking at.

The true benefits of wilderness must be earned. Access must be undemocratically difficult, and any intimacy with the place must come from your own experience, initiative, and resourcefulness, not from interpretive guidebooks.

The Virginia barrier islands are among the last that offer these challenges. To reach the islands, you must go by private boat, negotiating a maze of salt marsh channels and shallow bays. There are no facilities on the islands, so you must bring whatever you need to eat or drink. There are no lifeguards to protect you from dangerous riptides, no shelter from biting insects, no one to help push your boat off a sandbar should you beach it in the wrong spot, at the wrong tide. And should you become curious about the plants of the marsh and dunes; the birds of the bays and creeks; the reptiles, fish, insects; or the history and geology of the place, you must figure things out for yourself. There are no booklets, labels, videos, or tour leaders.

But experiencing the islands as wilderness is something more than a moderate physical and intellectual challenge that eliminates the casual visitors. To appreciate the islands as wilderness, one must see the challenge as part of the reward and must want the experience deeply enough to make some sacrifices. To some, a day alone paddling a canoe through a remote marsh or hiking a desolate beach would be boring, perhaps even an intimidating experience. For those who think otherwise, the experience can be restorative and strengthening. Not all of us want to have this experience, but for those of us who do, it is fortunate this one place remains.

Parramore

The story of how an island was saved

It could be said that we have the U.S. Navy to thank for saving the seaside islands, bays, and marshes of the Eastern Shore. On January 20, 1955, the *Peninsula Enterprise,* a weekly newspaper published in Accomac, reported that the navy was planning to take Parramore Island by condemnation and turn it into a bombing range. The owner of the island contacted George B. Fell, executive director of the Nature Conservancy, and asked for help in protecting the island. Although the navy eventually dropped plans for the bombing range, the conservancy's active involvement in protecting the islands had begun.

The air force had been using Wreck Island for target practice, but the Parramore proposal touched a number of sensitive issues, ranging from conservation to the local economy. According to newspaper accounts, the proposal was opposed by the local chamber of commerce and by watermen's groups because of the potential for damage to oyster beds and the recreational fishing business in the towns of Wachapreague and Quinby, just a few miles inland of Parramore Island. The newspaper also reported that some local people were in favor of the plan because they thought they could get jobs there, which conjures up the image of people running through the dunes with big bull's-eyes painted on their backs.

Conservationists opposed the plan because it would have caused extensive damage to one of the largest and most pristine islands in the coastal chain. Important also was the fact that the owners of the island, Mrs. Jean Saunders and her son Dr. Carl Schmidlapp, were conservationists who understood the damage the proposal would cause. Establishment of a bombing range would have required the clearing of two target areas, each of them six thousand feet in diameter, meaning virtual destruction of the maritime forest in the island interior. Other than Assateague, Parramore is the only barrier island with a significant stand of old-growth forest.

In February 1955 the conservancy was approached by Richard Hollerith, a friend of the Schmidlapps, who that April moved to a historic farm, Warwick, near Quinby, from his previous residence in New Jersey. George Fell promised to help fight the navy plan, and thus began the conservancy's relationship with the Schmidlapp family and Parramore Island.

In those days the Nature Conservancy had few members, no national recognition, and a very modest budget. Protection efforts were grass-root, mainly a letter-writing campaign and an effort to rally other conservation organizations and influential individuals. The conservancy's interest was in protecting the barrier islands as a wilderness area, as opposed to conveying them to the National Parks Service for public recreation.

After public opposition cooled the navy's interest in constructing a bombing range, efforts to protect the island continued. Dr. Richard H. Goodwin, the Nature Conservancy's president, contacted Dr. Schmidlapp in late 1957 and suggested the family donate a portion of the island each year to the conservancy. Dr. Schmidlapp replied that his attorneys recommended against the plan but emphasized that he would someday like to see the conservancy acquire the island, and he pledged not to sell it for "subdivision or real estate exploitation."

The conservancy board voted in August 1963 to purchase a three-month option on the island. The proposal called for eventual purchase, with Dr. Schmidlapp and his brother Horace given exclusive life tenancy. The conservancy would buy the island and then turn it over to a state or federal agency for use as a nature preserve. The Schmidlapps turned down the offer, preferring private management rather than state or federal ownership.

Negotiations were renewed when a *New York Times* article in February 1970 highlighted the growing likelihood of commercial development of the barrier islands. A New York company, Smith Island Development Corporation, had purchased Smith, Myrtle, and Ship Shoal Islands in late 1969, and it announced plans for a

$150 million resort and second-home community of up to 50,000 people.

The conservancy had been negotiating for other parcels in the island chain and in 1970 purchased 750-acre Godwin Island, an interior island northwest of Smith, with the financial aid of the Mary Flagler Cary Charitable Trust. The conservancy bought most of Hog Island in November 1970 and a month later announced that an agreement had been made with the Smith Island Development Corporation for their property, thus bringing to a formal closure the plans for a major resort development on the three southern-most islands.

Thomas Richards, then conservancy president, resumed negotiations with Dr. Schmidlapp and other members of the corporation who had become part owners of the island. At a meeting in June 1971 the primary stockholders of the corporation told Nature Conservancy representatives that disposal of the property would hinge upon three factors: the land must remain in its natural state, the corporation members must have use of the island for twenty years, and a sale must generate a satisfactory return for the stock-holders. It was agreed to have an independent appraisal made of the island.

An appraisal was completed during the fall, and contact was made with the Mary Flagler Cary Charitable Trust regarding the possibility of funding a purchase. In April 1972 conservancy vice president Pat Noonan met with principals of the corporation to discuss key provisions of an agreement. In April 1973 the conservancy board of governors approved a purchase agreement that would convey the island to the conservancy. The Schmidlapp group would have rights to the island for twenty years. The Cary Trust agreed to fund the project. While Parramore was not one of the first islands purchased by the Nature Conservancy, it was the most significant, with the largest maritime forest remaining in the island chain—the "crown jewel," said a 1973 news release.

Folly Creek Notebook

Living through seasons of change

A little bit of Folly Creek runs through my veins. I was born and raised not far from here. My father brought me to the creek to go fishing when I was barely old enough to walk. I nearly drowned in the inlet where the creek meets the ocean when I stepped off a sandbar and went in over my head. I still have an irrational fear of deep water.

I learned to kill here. My father and I hunted rails (a type of small wading bird) in the fall during high lunar tides, polling a small wooden skiff across the flooded salt marsh, flushing clapper rails from the grass and shooting enough for our family to have for dinner. Hunting still has for me a quality that is steeped in ritual— the taking of a life to nourish one's own. It is ancient and barbaric, but it is real. It was the directness of the process of life and death, the unbending reality of it, that made its impression upon me out on Folly Creek. My father and I went out in a flooding tide and killed birds for the family, much as a hawk might, or a fox, or, for that matter, a rail as it plucks a grasshopper from a blade of *spartina* grass.

I felt that I knew nature better by having participated in it, eliminating the cattle ranches, poultry farms, slaughterhouses, and grocery markets that turn the daily business of living and dying into a distant act of commerce. Like Isaac MacCaslin in Faulkner's *The Bear,* I had shed my first worthy blood, and I was proud.

Years later, I was on Folly Creek with my family as my father lay dying. He had suffered an aortic aneurysm and was in the hospital, and the surgeons kept him alive long enough for us to rush to the emergency room to say good-bye. So Folly Creek has been with us through youth and old age, through birth and death, through sadness and times of great joy and discovery.

Folly Creek has changed over the years, as have the islands, inlet, and bays it flows through. The creek begins as a trickle near the town of Accomac, draining farmland and forest, and it gradually widens and deepens and becomes tidal, meandering through salt marshes, and finally emptying into Metompkin Inlet, which separates Metompkin and Cedar Islands.

When I was growing up, the inlet was about one-half mile south of its present location. It was deep enough for large boats to navigate, and a coast guard station on the north end of Cedar Island regularly sent rescue boats through the inlet to assist boaters at sea. But gradually the inlet grew shallow, the coast guard station closed, and a sandbar began to spread between Cedar and Metompkin Islands. In a few years the inlet closed completely, and the islands grew together. Folly Creek, needing an outlet to the ocean, bore through a low area on Metompkin Island, creating a new inlet. The old part of the creek, behind Cedar Island, is gradually filling in and becoming salt marsh. We were out in the little skiff the other day in a part of the creek that once was more than twenty feet deep, when we struck bottom. The water was about six inches deep.

※ ※ ※

So change is the nature of things here in these inlets and islands. The sand of these islands seems organic, with a life of its own, forever changing like an amoeba, constantly altering itself in response to pressures from outside the organism. In this particular place, given the kinetic energy of the ocean and the inertia of land, change is a matter of survival. The islands change daily, by the minute, by the second. Sand is slowly carried from the continental shelf toward the mainland and is deposited as offshore bars. Waves carry sand as they break upon the beach, and because waves usually strike the land at an angle, a longshore current is created that moves sand parallel to the beach in what is called littoral drift. On most of the East Coast, the drift moves in a north–south direction, carrying sand from northern islands to southern ones.

While sand is constantly being moved by wave action and the longshore current, wind also has an effect, building and erasing dunes or helping to feed the longshore current by sending dry sand into the ocean with offshore breezes.

These three elements—sea, sand, and wind—work together to create something of a dynamic balance. The topography of barrier islands is never fixed; change is a natural part of the process, and as the islands change, the mainland is protected, especially during storms, when a great deal of energy is concentrated in a small area, over a relatively brief time.

During northeast storms or hurricanes, new inlets can be cut between barrier islands and existing inlets can be closed, dunes can be flattened by both wind and water, and entire islands can be temporarily converted into sandbars. While the immediate effects may appear devastating, such alterations in the landscape are the islands' means of absorbing the energy of the ocean, especially when it is magnified by storm tides, heavy seas, and strong winds.

It is the nature of the islands to constantly change their profile, much to the frustration of cartographers and mariners, who prefer their channels and coastal inlets to stay put for a reasonable length of time. But the islands are alive in the sense that they respond to what is around them, which always is the sea and frequently is the product of humans.

The barrier islands are like a giant rubber buffer that separates a force in motion—the sea—from an object at rest—the land. By acquiescing to the forces of the sea, by changing and flowing with the sea's energy as if it were water itself, the islands survive and thus protect the object at rest from the kinetic force.

Geologists call the phenomenon island migration; others call it erosion. If someone builds a house on an island, intending it to be more or less permanent, they will find that sooner or later the island will squirm out from under it, leaving it at the mercy of the sea. The builder must then move the house to the island's new address and be prepared to repeat the process every few years.

Building on beaches is a relatively new phenomenon. The American Indians, who seemed to have a superior understanding of the sea's edge, built their villages in the forested uplands, well removed from the daily Sturm und Drang of the three elements. Early settlers, perhaps taking a lesson from the Indians, built their residences in the upland and used the islands as pastures for cattle and horses, no fencing required. It was not until the Civil War era that we decided that the hostility of the sea edge was no match for American technology; we wanted to live on the beach, so we would tame those elements that our grandfathers feared and respected.

The battle has raged for a century and a half. The sea edge insists on being dynamic, while we demand that it stay in one place for a reasonable length of time. Although we have fought a good fight, victory has yet eluded us.

Often, if enough houses are built on an island, it becomes easier and cheaper to put sand under the houses rather than moving the houses to where the sand happens to be. In resort cities along the coast, taxpayers spend millions of dollars to fund beach replenishment projects, in which huge pumps suck sand from the bottom of the Atlantic and deposit it along the developed beachfront.

And on resort beaches, more millions in taxpayers' dollars are used to hire bulldozers to build tall sand dunes to separate the beach from the houses, hotels, and other businesses. The dunes give property owners a great feeling of security, those sandy, manmade mountains protecting them from the petulance of the sea. But they find, after a rigorous northeast storm, that the ocean can reduce their mountains to overwash fans in the space of a single high tide cycle. And that, of course, is what the islands intended all along; any man-made mountain of sand near the surf zone is by definition temporary.

※　※　※

Barrier beaches have survived for all of these centuries not by challenging the ocean, but by accommodating it. Wild beaches and offshore bars, such as those along the Virginia coast, are low, wide, and dynamic, and when a storm hits, its energy is dissipated over a wide expanse of low beach. The ocean flows over the island, flattening temporary dunes, carrying nutrients to the leeward salt marshes, creating vast shell-laden plains where in the spring, terns and plovers will nest.

Barrier beaches are unstable by design. Sand moves as readily as the water and wind, and to stop the beaches from moving is as pointless as trying to halt the ocean current or stop the wind from blowing.

In a natural barrier island and estuarine system, the only constant is an elemental balance, which is tested daily by sea level and the pulse of the tides. On the beach, every inch counts. In a storm, an area a few inches lower than its surroundings might become an overwash fan; and if the storm is persistent and violent, it might even become a new inlet. An area a few inches higher than its surroundings might support a stand of beach grass, which will trap sand and encourage the area to grow even higher, becoming a small dune. An area a few inches higher than its surroundings will provide safe nesting areas for colonies of plovers, terns, and skimmers. Birds that build in low areas are likely to lose their eggs or chicks to high tides should there be a storm during the nesting cycle.

The changing nature of barrier beaches is easily seen. A swim in the surf provides immediate evidence. You place your beach towel and sunglasses on the berm of the beach, dive into the breakers, tread water for a few minutes, and find that you have moved several dozen yards south from where you placed your towel and glasses and entered the water. Your trip was courtesy of the longshore current, which, while it transported you along the beach, was providing the same service for billions and billions of grains of sand, many of which have by now found their way into your swimsuit.

If you swim back to the beach and retrieve your towel, you'll find that it is gritty with sand, thanks to the breeze that keeps those tiny crystals of quartz and feldspar moving along. If the wind was really blowing, your towel would be completely covered with sand and you might not even find it until the wind changed direction and began herding the grains of sand to another destination.

The islands change constantly, and these changes manifest themselves in both near-term and long-term ways. A swimmer can feel the nudge of the longshore current, the sting of blowing sand. Those of us who spend a lot of time on the beach can see the seasonal metamorphosis: the widening of the berm in summer, the narrowing in winter as sand is carried by storms from the beach to the offshore bars, the islands' first line of defense. But it requires all of our imagination to see the long-term adjustments of the islands, their migrations, their fluidlike tendencies to roll and flow, which seem more closely related to a field of molten lava than fastland.

Imagine a satellite camera focused on the chain of barrier islands. Each month the camera clicks off a frame. Over several decades, if we join the frames to make a movie, we'll have a brief midterm view of barrier island behavior. Assuming sea level continues to rise, many of the islands will appear to roll over backward as storms dump sand leeward of the dune line, covering existing marshes, forming new beaches west of the old ones, which will become offshore bars. Some islands will appear to spin, like a propeller, eroding on the south end and accreting on the north, then reversing the process. Inlets will close, and new ones will open. Islands will join together, and new islands will be formed.

If our satellite camera keeps clicking away as the next few centuries unfold, we'll have created an engrossing drama that includes such major characters as sea level change, glacial melt, and global warming. It's easy to see the daily, monthly, and even yearly changes in barrier island topography, but most of us still think of the larger universe as being more or less static. Of course, it is not. Changes are simply measured on a calendar with a different scale.

Over many centuries of monthly satellite photos, we'll see that not only do the islands change, but their setting changes. The glaciers melt and sea level rises, covering much of the land. There still will be barrier islands and salt marshes, but they will gradually move farther and farther west as the sea level slowly rises. One day, we will reach a point when the sea level peaks and then slowly begins its ebb. Polar temperatures will cool slightly, glaciers will again rob the oceans of seawater, and the barrier beaches will begin another migration, this time eastward, toward the receding sea. It has been so for as long as anyone has been keeping score. Ice ages are not simply chapters in ancient history, but part of the evolution of planet earth—a tidal cycle, as it were, on a scale larger than we're used to. Instead of measuring in hours, we must think in terms of centuries, or hundreds of centuries.

In the past 1.8 million years the sea level has risen and fallen six times. The last Great Low Tide began its ebb about 35,000 years ago and receded for more than 20,000 years. When the tide finally began to turn, the sea level was 400 feet lower than it is today, and the Atlantic beaches were some 60 miles east of where they are now, on the continental shelf.

Fifteen thousand years ago huge glaciers scoured the continents, pressing north and south from the poles like invading armies, changing forever the landscapes through which they marched. In North America, the last great glacier, the Laurentide, scraped its way southward to what is now New York and New Jersey. Where the glaciers marched, the coast is rocky and rugged, scrubbed of its layer of sand and topsoil. The Laurentide glacier drew southward as far as Long Island, whose north coast shows its rocky, glaciated past, and whose south shore has the flat, sandy beaches common to the unglaciated coast.

While the coast south of New York and New Jersey was spared the last glacier, the beaches we walk upon today are glacial products, bits and pieces of the Appalachians, ground and weathered, washed into the ocean when the great ice sheets began melting twelve to fifteen thousand years ago. So our sand is indeed ancient, bits and pieces of earth that once lay far west of us and were washed from the highlands to the sea, then lay on the sea floor for centuries more before finally being nudged by the energy of the Atlantic back to shore.

The sea level today continues to rise, as it has for the past twelve thousand years. In some future century, we will reach the high tide portion of the cycle, and the seas will again begin their inexorable ebb as glaciers begin to build. Of course, this is a simplified explanation of a very complex and gradual cycle. Something could happen—global warming, nuclear war—and there would be no next ice age, or it would be delayed substantially. The sea would continue to rise and the barrier islands would continue to migrate westward, to the foothills of the Appalachians.

Human life, in time measured by glaciers, is less than the blink of an eye. The rise and fall of glacial tides is so gradual it seems not to occur at all, so we tend to think of the land in terms of permanence, of stability, even though it actually is slowly shuffling under our feet. The "erosion" of coastal areas is not necessarily an aberration, a symptom of something gone wrong, but evidence of another tick of the geological clock.

Perhaps the best advice for those wishing to live on the ocean could be given by the American Indians and the early European settlers, who hunted and fished on the beaches but built their homes in the safety of upland forests. They knew that the sea was coming, and when it did, they would at least have a good head start.

Spartina

Getting to know the swamp creature

I was in the aluminum johnboat, winding my way through Knocknees Gut, which is a shortcut between Folly Creek and Longboat Channel. In the taxonomy of the seaside, a gut is smaller than a creek but wider than a drain, which is pronounced "dreen." In the distance I could see the fishing village of Wachapreague, and farther eastward were Parramore Island and Cedar Island. Tom and I have a duck blind on a bend in Knocknees, and I wanted to check on it before the season got under way. The blind is nothing fancy. We built a frame out of some leftover four-by-four posts and some two-by-fours, and then we stretched dog pen wire around the framework. Early each fall we cut cedar boughs and stick them in the openings in the wire, and in an hour or so we have what a duck might consider a large cedar bush growing out in the center of the marsh.

We do the duck population of Knocknees little harm. We've taken a few buffleheads and hooded mergansers, but the more desirable black ducks are too smart to go anywhere near a cedar bush growing where no other cedar bushes grow. The last time we went duck hunting, we left the house well before dawn, having loaded the boat the evening before. Driving to the launch site, I had the nagging feeling that I had forgotten some vital item of duck hunting paraphernalia. When we reached the blind and began setting up, I realized I had left the decoys at home. I had taken the box of decoys out of the boat when we went clamming a few days earlier. It's difficult to lure ducks to your blind without decoys, so Tom and I walked the marsh and enjoyed watching the sun slowly appear over Cedar Island, bathing the salt marsh in warm gold morning light.

Duck hunting is an excuse to get out in the marsh in winter, when sane people are at home in a warm bed, or having hotcakes and country sausage at the local restaurant. The older I get, the less driven I am to shoot ducks. Yet, I enjoy the experience of being out there, of hiking the high marsh, which is like no other hiking on earth.

I enjoy hiking mountain trails, but they don't compare to walking a vast marshland, where I can see for miles across a sea of green *spartina,* finding treasures that the last storm tide washed up, having the place totally to myself. I must admit, few people share my passion for marshes. When people go for hikes, even here on the coast, they seldom go on the marsh.

We've been taught in our culture to avoid marshes and swamps. There is something sinister about a marsh, something forbidding. People distrust places where the footing is not always solid and reliable. We like dependability and certainty; we like knowing what to expect when we put our feet down.

Marshes have been unfairly maligned in our society for centuries. I think of bad guys in old Tarzan movies who sink forever into swampy mud pits. There's the image of Humphrey Bogart covered with leeches in *The African Queen. Swamp Thing. The Creature from the Swamp* . . . Nothing good comes from a marsh, only evil and death. Marshes are filled with poisonous snakes, disease-carrying insects, foul smells, and labyrinthine waterways where one can become lost forever.

Such attitudes, still widely held and perpetuated in our culture, helped bring about the destruction of hundreds of thousands of acres of marshlands in America during the last century. Marshlands were wasteland, and to conquer it—to reclaim it as farmland, homesite, garbage dump, or industrial park—was a noble undertaking. In fine American tradition, we took something of no worth, and through hard work and perseverance, we made it useful and productive.

As the legal debate over protecting tidal marshes raged in the 1970s, scientists produced numerous studies demonstrating the remarkable fecundity and usefulness of a marsh. We now know that the biomass produced annually by a natural marsh rivals that of America's most fertile and chemically manipulated farmland. Marshes are responsible for millions of dollars worth of fish and shellfish, which support coastal economies and help feed the world. Marshes protect the mainland from storms. Marshes filter contaminants from surface water and return it to aquifers in a purer state.

To provide legal protection to salt marshes, it was necessary to prove that they offer substantial tangible benefits to humans, that they do their part in our free market economy, providing food, jobs, clean water, recreation, and flood protection. Few arguments were made that marshes should be protected because of their inherent beauty, their biological diversity, or because they represent the last of the coastal wilderness in the mid-Atlantic.

The wilderness value of a vast salt marsh is no less, it seems to me, than the mountain ranges of the west, which normally come to mind when someone speaks of wilderness. But the same arguments for preserving mountain ranges as wilderness can also be applied to salt marshes. Indeed, a salt marsh wilderness is more fragile and vulnerable, its subtle beauty more easily marred than that of mountains. The highest value of a natural salt marsh lies in its wildness, its ability to offer momentary escape from the world humans have created, a place where nature is in control. I enjoy hiking a marsh, or canoeing its creeks, because it provides the same surprises, the same sense of discovery, as any other wilderness setting.

The vegetated marsh is surprisingly firm, its dark soil knitted by the complex roots of cordgrass, *Spartina alterniflora,* the dominant plant species of coastal marshes throughout the United States. The soil is also matted with the decaying leaves and stems of *spartina,* especially in the higher marshes, where the tides reach only now and then to sweep away plant litter. Underfoot, there are ribbed mussels, growing in clusters amid the roots of *spartina.* And there is *Salicornia,* or saltwort, a tubular, succulent little plant that the old-timers used to pickle in vinegar to use as a relish. Dark gray fiddler crabs, the males waving one huge claw in a phallic advertisement, scurry through the grass and disappear into burrows. Marsh periwinkles crawl up the stalks of *spartina,* scraping nutrients from the surface of the grass. And you find surprises: a broken shell of a willet egg, tan and spotted with brown and purple; the carapace of a horseshoe crab; a midden of shells left by oystercatchers in a favorite feeding spot; the nest of a clapper rail in the high grass on the edge of a creek; shiny black egg casings of skates, called mermaid's purses; and chains of egg casings of channeled whelks, which look from a distance like the discarded skin of a snake.

What you don't find in the marsh are mutant swamp creatures, evil-smelling gases, venomous reptiles, and plague-carrying insects. A healthy marsh smells good, the odor of a giant food factory at work: photosynthesis, cell division, cell decay, the attack of bacteria on cellulose, egg production, egg consumers, millions of

Salt marsh cordgrass
(Spartina alterniflora)

M. A. CLARKE

larvae, countless millions of new lives, deaths, transformations, the sharing of energy, the passing of life from plant to animal, from animal to plant, the sustenance and substance of life.

* * *

The marshes do have their mysteries. How, for example, is a grass such as *spartina* able to survive in an environment that would bring quick death to nearly any other plant? *Spartina* seems to thrive on the saltwater of the estuary, growing tallest and thickest along the edges of creeks, where its roots are immersed twice daily, its stems washed by the flowing tides. It is a remarkable plant, irrigated by pure seawater, engineered to withstand violent coastal storms, a processor and distributor of solar energy upon which the entire estuary depends.

On the salt marsh, *Spartina alterniflora* is ubiquitous. Along the edges of creeks and bays, it grows in thick stands, sometimes to heights of six feet. On the upper marsh, where tidal flow is limited, the grass is shorter, from about six inches to two or three feet, and it grows less dense, often with colonies of *Salicornia*. In the upper elevations, where the salt marsh joins fastland, *Spartina alterniflora* gives way to *Spartina patens*, a shorter, thicker grass called salt-meadow hay, and *Dichtylis spicata*, or salt grass.

The entire community of marshes, bays, islands, fish, shellfish, birds, and animals begins here with these grasses that form the basis of the salt marsh food chain, collecting the energy of the sun in photosynthesis, and later distributing it to myriad creatures as the grasses die and are broken down by bacteria. The mixture of bacteria, epiphytic algae, and the cellulose particles of digested *spartina* form the broad base of the salt marsh food chain, a nutrient-rich soup called detritus.

It is a remarkable but very economical process perfected over centuries of natural selection. Nothing is superfluous. Nothing is left to waste. The system is fragile but perfectly balanced. The plants grow prodigiously during the summer, fed by nutrients swept in with the tides, storing the energy of the sun through photosynthesis during the long, unshaded days. Then in the fall this stored energy is released as the exposed stems and leaves die. The plant collapses to the marsh floor, and the bacteria attack. The single-cell bacteria are so small they cannot consume bits of *spartina* in the traditional manner. Instead, the plant is digested outside the cells of the animals, and as a result, the *spartina* is reduced to progressively smaller bits and pieces.

This rich detritus mixture—bacteria, plant remains, larvae, free-flowing eggs, and algae stirred by tidal action into a nutritious broth—is eaten by protozoans that live in the shallow water, by the filter-feeding burrowing worms of the tidal flats, by oysters, clams, mussels, nematodes, snails, insect larva, fiddler crabs, and small fish such as menhaden and mullet, which either filter the nutrients from the water or eat them with bottom mud.

Clams burrow beneath the bottom and send up a pair of siphons, one of which pulls detritus-rich seawater through its digestive system, while the other expels small, nondigestible particles and waste. Most of the filter feeders consume detritus in this manner, sucking the broth through hairlike cilia, through membranes, or, in the case of the marsh mussel, through a mesh of mucous threads covering its gills.

Fiddler crabs eat detritus by picking up gobs of it with their claws, then sorting out the digestible particles with six specially adapted legs that cover their mouths. The tiny legs are shaped like paddles and are covered with stiff bristles, which sort the large particles of food from the small. The small particles are digested, but the larger pieces are temporarily stored in a predigestive chamber, and when they accumulate are spit back into a claw and returned to the surface of the marsh.

If you hike a high marsh or walk along an exposed tidal flat, you will see several species of snails. Mud snails forage along the surface of the flat, scraping detritus from the surface with their radulae, rasplike teeth, which pull food particles into their mouths. The marsh periwinkle feeds on the lower stems of *spartina*, scraping away algae and detritus that has collected on the plant.

The detritus eaters are preyed upon by animals higher on the food chain: larger fish, blue crabs, waterfowl, wading birds, raccoons, and other mammals. A clapper rail stalks the cordgrass marsh, spearing an unsuspecting periwinkle snail from a grass stem. A great blue heron waits patiently in a shallow gut, then surprises a passing killifish. An osprey circles over the open creek, dives, and comes up with a mullet in its talons. A fisherman drifts in a small boat along a tidal creek, hoping to entice a flounder with an offering of squid and minnows.

Sound Beach

Of life, death, and terrapin stew

The diamondback terrapin had laid her clutch of eggs at the foot of a shallow dune and was lumbering back to the bay, her shell covered with sand. We watched her enter the water, and then followed her footprints to where she had deposited her eggs. They were buried beneath the sand, well hidden to our eyes, but predators were all around.

The dunes were marked with the footprints of raccoons, and we found fox prints in a path between the dunes and the salt marsh. Fish crows were patrolling the marsh, and they could make quick work of terrapin eggs. How many, we wondered, would survive?

Lynn and Tom and I were hiking a Chesapeake Bay natural area called Sound Beach, which lies between Onancock Creek and Back Creek on the Eastern Shore. The beach, and Parker's Marsh behind it, form a low-lying peninsula, or "neck," nearly surrounded by water.

In early summer it is a beautiful place. The beach is narrow, separated from the salt marsh by small dunes, and now and then by sandy flats where high tides breached the dunes and carried sand several yards into the marsh. If you stand on the dunes and look toward the mainland, you will see meandering creeks and shallow ponds, meadows of emerald *spartina,* and dark, spiked grasses called black needlerush. Here and there are small forested islands called hammocks, where a few inches of additional elevation allow pines and cedars to grow.

There are dozens of these hammocks along the bay on the northern part of Virginia's Eastern Shore. Farther south, the bay meets the upland with very little marshy fringe to separate water from fastland, but here the salt marsh stretches for miles, peppered here and there by hammocks, whose tall pines are favorite nesting sites of bald eagles. If you look at the hammocks on a topographical map, many will appear as semicircular ridges, indicating that at one time they were part of a Carolina bay, a small swampy area surrounded by upland.

You need a boat to get to most of the bayside hammocks and to Sound Beach. We left the town of Onancock in our little skiff, followed the red and green channel markers, and in about fifteen minutes beached the boat at Ware Point, which is on the southern tip of the peninsula. From there we hiked around the tip and northward up the beach, pausing now and then to look for beach treasures, or to enjoy the view across Parker's Marsh toward the mainland.

Diamondback terrapin

Turtle eggs caught our eye long before we saw the diamondback plodding across the beach. Not long after we began our hike, we found a nest of spent eggs, a dozen or more of them. The shells were leathery, each with a slit from end to end, through which the hatchling escaped. They were in a shallow depression in the sand on the side of a small dune, only a few yards from the water.

We found many other spent shells scattered along the beach, evidence that the population of diamondback terrapins is doing well here at Sound Beach. It hasn't always been that way. The terrapin today has its predators—raccoons and fish crows most notably—but humans once ranked high on the list, and in the early 1900s the population nearly was wiped out.

Coastal residents have eaten terrapins since the Native Americans taught colonists how to bake them over a fire. Indeed, the word "terrapin" is an Algonquian Indian term meaning "edible turtle." Until the early 1900s, terrapin stew was a staple of most coastal households. *Housekeeper's Companion* (New York: J. B. Alden), an 1889 collection of favorite recipes of Eastern Shore cooks compiled by Bessie Gunter, goes into gruesome detail on the craft of dismantling a terrapin. May Gunter suggested that when preparing terrapin stew, one should first let the animal swim in cold water for three or four hours to cleanse it. Then, it should be plunged head-first into a pot of boiling water, covered, and cooked until the skin can be easily removed from the feet. Miss Gunter recommended cooking the meat in butter and cream and seasoning with salt and pepper.

Another contributor, Miss Corson, favored a more complex sauce. She began by making a roux, browning flour in a bit of butter, and then added cream while stirring. The terrapin meat was added to the cream base, which was seasoned with salt, cayenne pepper, and nutmeg. Just before serving, Miss Corson added the beaten yolks of four eggs, one gill of Madeira wine, and a tablespoon of lemon juice.

Terrapins got into trouble in the late 1800s when terrapin stew became a fad in big-city restaurants. Nearly ninety thousand pounds of terrapins were caught in the Chesapeake Bay region in 1891, and some enterprising early aquaculturists even operated terrapin farms, where diamondbacks were raised for market.

At the peak of their popularity, diamondback terrapins were selling for $30 to $120 per dozen, depending upon their size. The largest and most valuable were mature females, and when the number of breeding females dropped, the population crashed.

The terrapin stew fad lasted as long as the terrapins did. They were greatly overfished, and by 1920 the annual catch was down to about eight hundred pounds, and the diamondback terrapin was

in danger of being wiped out. Laws were passed to protect the terrapin, and the diamondback slowly began its recovery.

While the diamondback terrapin population has recovered, it
most likely will never regain its prominence at the family dining
table. "One hundred years before New York knew the terrapin, it
was daily food in Accawmacke [Accomack County]," John S. Wise
wrote in 1899 in *The End of an Era* (Boston: Houghton Mifflin).
Fortunately for the terrapin, the era of terrapin stew laced with
Madeira seems to have come to its end.

※ ※ ※

Diamondback terrapins are plentiful in the little creeks that meander through these wide marshes around Sound Beach. While exploring an unnamed creek by canoe one day, I sat still for a few
minutes and let the current take me where it would. Soon, little
heads began to break the surface of the water, and just under the
surface I could make out the muted golden color of the shell and
its distinctive pattern that gives the terrapin its name. There must
have been dozens of them in a small creek about eight feet wide.

While terrapins spend most of their lives in the shallow bays
and creeks of the salt marsh, the females go ashore in summer to
lay eggs in the dunes above the high tide line.

Terrapins reproduce when the males are six to ten years old and
the females are between eight and thirteen. Female terrapins measure up to eight inches in length and are larger than males, which
grow to only five inches. They always mate in the water, usually at
night.

The female lays her eggs in a shallow nest and covers them with
sand. The eggs hatch in sixty to one hundred days, and the young
turtles are about one inch long when they emerge from the shell
and make their way back toward the water. The temperature in the
nest is believed to determine the sex of the hatchlings. At higher
temperatures, more females develop. At lower temperatures, more
males develop.

Terrapins, like most turtles, live for a long time. Most live to be
at least forty years old, and some much longer. Most turtles spend

their adult lives in the same stretch of water. Researchers in South Carolina tagged diamondbacks and retrieved 442 turtles a year or more after they had been tagged. All but 25 were found in the same area of the same creek where they had originally been tagged. The female seems willing to travel only when she is ready to lay eggs. Then she will swim up to three miles to find a suitable stretch of sandy beach to deposit her eggs.

While diamondback terrapins survived the terrapin stew craze of the last century, threats today are less obvious. Small, young terrapins enter crab traps and drown, and waterfront development along the East Coast has greatly reduced the nesting areas available to terrapins. In populated beach areas, automobiles take a deadly toll on terrapins when they come ashore and cross a highway trying to find a suitable nesting site.

The stretch of Sound Beach, then, seems special. We have miles of sandy beach with a gentle berm, no roads and no houses. It's a perfect nesting habitat, and just beyond the beach are tidal creeks and shallow ponds where diamondback terrapins can live comfortably for forty years or more. Call it terrapin heaven.

North Landing River

A wind tide on a green sea

An old folk song called "Erie Canal" begins with the words "Low bridge, everybody down." We were approaching a low bridge across a tributary of the North Landing River, and we figured that if we flattened ourselves in the bottom of the boat, we would make it through. The bottom of the bridge was slowly passing overhead, inches from our faces, when we discovered an unforeseen dilemma. The outboard motor forgot to duck.

The shiny new Honda met the façade of the bridge and came away with an abrasion the color of concrete. Mary Kathryn van Eerden alertly shifted the motor into reverse. But the shiny new four-stroke had just gotten its first battle scar.

It was clearly an issue of either the bridge being too low, or the tide being too high. In any case, it provided Mary Kathryn the opportunity to tell Lynn and Tom and me about wind tides, which create a unique ecosystem along the North Landing River in southern Virginia Beach.

"Most people think of tides as being lunar," she said. "The water is pushed and pulled by the gravity of the moon, and every six hours or so we have low and high tides. But because of its location at the northern end of a chain of several large bodies of water, the tides on the North Landing are influenced by wind. If the wind is from the south, the water is pushed into the river. If it is from the north, it is pushed out. So the tide doesn't change until the wind does."

The phenomenon of wind tides has created a community of plants and animals that have adapted to this quirk of geography. "It's one of the best examples in the world of an irregular wind tide ecosystem," said Mary Kathryn. "There are fifty-two rare or endangered plant and animal species here. It truly is a unique landscape."

Mary Kathryn and her husband, Brian, both work for the Nature Conservancy, which has been interested in protecting this corner of southeast Virginia since 1973, when the conservancy worked with the Union Camp Corporation to arrange a gift of forty-nine thousand acres to the Department of the Interior to create the Great Dismal Swamp National Wildlife Refuge. More recently, the conservancy has worked with the federal government, the state, the cities of Virginia Beach and Chesapeake, and private landowners to create corridors of undeveloped land that connect large tracts such as Dismal Swamp, Back Bay, and Mackay Island in North Carolina. This corner of southeast Virginia includes a wealth of rare species, from red-cockaded woodpeckers to insect-eating orchids.

The project is called Green Sea, a new turn on a term that was applied to the region several centuries ago. "When William Byrd surveyed the Virginia-Carolina line in 1729, he looked out over the area when approaching from the west and saw thousands of acres of cane blowing in the breeze," said Mary Kathryn. "He wrote in his journal that it looked like a vast green sea, and that term stuck. If you look at old maps, you'll see Great Dismal Swamp and Green Sea used to describe the area."

In those days it was a green sea that seemed without limit, stretching all the way from the coast along Back Bay westward to encompass the Dismal Swamp and Lake Drummond, and southward to the pocosins (upland swamps) and shallow lakes of North Carolina. The swamp has shrunken a bit over the years, with much of the Dismal Swamp having been drained to create farmland, and with subdivisions and shopping malls popping up on many tracts of William Byrd's Green Sea.

But there still remains an awful lot of Green Sea in this rural corner of southeast Virginia and northeast North Carolina. In a small boat on the North Landing River, it's easy to appreciate Byrd's image. The North Landing stretches for some twenty-two miles from the North Carolina line northward into Virginia Beach, where it becomes the Albemarle and Chesapeake Canal at the

North Landing drawbridge. The river is wide where we were, near Munden Point Park, with North Carolina just a short distance away. On a summer morning the river was hazy and flat, and along its edge great meadows of grass stretched to the forest on the horizon.

When the bridge interrupted our exploration of one tributary, we continued northward and found others to investigate. The river is part of the Intracoastal Waterway system, and a regular flotilla of cabin cruisers and sailboats was parading by. Just past the Pungo Ferry Road Bridge we found an oxbow and left the river traffic for some quiet time in shallow water.

We poled the boat up a narrow stream until we could pole no farther. Pickerelweed was blooming, and swamp roses were growing in the higher areas. Wild celery, which looks a little like Queen Anne's lace, grew near the water. Cordgrass was green and lush, punctuated by the dark, sharp leaves of black needlerush.

Farther along North Landing we turned west into Pocaty River, and the landscape changed from open water and marsh to cypress swamp. Trees hung over the river, warblers crossed in front of us, and ospreys circled overhead. We went upriver until deadfalls made further progress impossible, and then returned to the junction of the Pocaty and North Landing. An observation platform has been built on the marsh here, a good place to stop for lunch and stretch the legs.

Seen from atop the platform, the Green Sea stretched for miles, the North Landing River helping to define the eastern boundary of it. "The North Landing and its marshes are a natural corridor," explained Mary Kathryn. "We have a great land base in wildlife refuges in the region, and this area links them. By protecting the North Landing we're protecting an even broader landscape."

* * *

On an early morning, well before dawn, I met with Mary Kathryn and Brian at a hunt club near the town of Wakefield. We planned to be out in the pine forest at first light, so after a quick cup of coffee and a doughnut we set off for the woods, with a purple sky

quickly fading to magenta. Thirty feet up in a large pine tree sat a
red-cockaded woodpecker, trapped by a wire screen in his nesting
cavity, tapping impatiently at the opening. From below, we could
see movement, a head bobbing up and down. At exactly four minutes after seven, we knew the time had come.

Brian van Eerden yanked a yellow cord, and the wire screen
tore free from the pine. The woodpecker took off like a missile,
whistling loudly, if a bit off key. Fifty yards away, Don Schwab
yanked another yellow cord, and a second woodpecker took flight.
The birds did not fly far, which was good. Brian and Don were acting as matchmakers. They wanted these woodpeckers to get to
know each other.

On that morning, six red-cockaded woodpeckers were released
in a remote pinewoods. At that moment, Virginia's population of
this endangered bird rose by 25 percent.

In the time of John James Audubon, red-cockaded woodpeckers were common in the southeastern United States, ranging from
New Jersey to Virginia and the Carolinas to Florida and Texas. But
these woodpeckers depend upon old-growth pine forests for survival, and by the mid-1900s this habitat had been reduced by more
than 95 percent. The bird went on the endangered species list in
1970, and in Virginia fewer than twenty individuals survived. Like
the larger ivory-billed woodpecker, the little red-cockaded seemed
headed for extinction.

But that might not happen just yet. Through a cooperative
effort involving federal and state wildlife agencies, conservation
organizations, and private landowners, the red-cockaded woodpecker is being reintroduced, and more important, habitat is being
managed in ways that may ensure the long-term survival of the
bird.

The relocation project involved a broad range of conservation
interests. South Carolina has a stable population of red-cockaded
woodpeckers, so the six birds were trapped at Sandhills National
Wildlife Refuge by Don Schwab of the Virginia Department of
Game and Inland Fisheries and Bryan Watts of the Center for
Conservation Biology (CCB) at the College of William and Mary.

They were taken to Piney Grove, a forest preserve of about twenty-seven hundred acres near Wakefield owned by the Nature Conservancy. Staging area for the project was the Waid's Corner Hunt Club, a Piney Grove neighbor.

"It was a team effort," said Brian van Eerden, who works as a stewardship ecologist with the conservancy. "Fish and Wildlife had the birds, the state game department had the method, CCB had the expertise, and the conservancy had the land. Hopefully, we can come back in a year and find that the birds have created families and are raising another generation of young."

The conservancy had red-cockaded woodpeckers in mind when it bought Piney Grove preserve from Hancock Timber Resource Group in 1998. The site had plenty of large pines, extensive forested areas, and Virginia's remaining population of nesting red-cockaded woodpeckers. The conservancy began managing the land for woodpeckers by selectively burning underbrush, removing hardwoods, and thinning mid-story growth.

The relocation project involved more than simply trapping birds and moving them a few hundred miles to a new home. Although red-cockaded woodpeckers were using the tract and had built clusters of nesting cavities, additional cavities were needed for the new birds. So the team built boxes of cedar and then inserted them in pine trees twenty to thirty feet off the ground. Holes were cut in the pines with a chainsaw, the boxes were inserted and cemented in place with epoxy, and in the end they were nearly identical to a cavity actually built by a bird.

The birds were captured late in the evening in South Carolina after they had gone to roost. They were fed live crickets hourly through the next day, and on the second evening they were released into their new homes and were kept overnight in the cavities by wire screens covering the opening.

"These birds are very social, they live in groups, so the idea was to release all of them at the same time early in the morning, when they normally would begin their day of foraging," said Brian. "Hopefully, they'll interact with each other and with native birds and form a colony."

As scientists have studied these endangered birds, they have learned more and more about the complex social interaction of red-cockaded woodpeckers. Groups of birds live in clusters of nesting trees within a circle about fifteen hundred feet in diameter. The red-cockaded is the only woodpecker to build its cavity in live pine trees. It prefers trees that are sixty to seventy years or older, and the cavity is excavated in the heartwood. Heartwood is usually very hard, so the birds look for trees that have a heartwood fungus called red heart, which weakens this nonliving fiber.

Around the cavity the birds chip away small holes called resin wells, and the sap from these holes coats the tree and protects the cavity from predators such as rat snakes. Older cavity trees will have large areas that are white with resin.

Red-cockaded woodpecker

Red-cockaded woodpeckers are what scientists call "cooperative breeders" in that the entire family helps raise the young. A family group consists of a breeding male and female, as well as several males from previous breeding seasons. These "helper" males incubate eggs, feed the young, construct new cavities, and help defend the group's territory. At the death of the breeding male, a younger male will usually take over that role. Young females usually leave the nest to begin family groups of their own.

"We are managing Piney Grove for red-cockaded woodpeckers, but in reality this is management on a broader scale," said Brian. "The conservancy's larger goal is conservation of the southern pine forest ecosystem, to which the woodpeckers are closely linked. Working on woodpecker recovery at Piney Grove engages the organization in fire and timber management, issues that influence biodiversity across the entire southeast. The woodpecker is a keystone species, a barometer of how well we are managing our land. The issue is not simply endangered birds, but diversity and a healthy ecosystem."

※　※　※

The Green Sea of southeast Virginia may have more statewide rare and endangered plant and animal species than any other part of the state. The reason is that the area represents the northern limit of the range of many plants and animals. We see things here we simply don't see elsewhere in the state.

The most dramatic example would be the longleaf pine, a tree that literally is a part of Virginia history but is rarely seen in the state anymore. The only place it can be found is here in some sandy soil that in ancient times was part of a dune system a stone's throw from the ocean.

When European settlers first arrived, they found thousands of acres of longleaf pine in parklike forests across southeastern Virginia. The great trees did not fare well as the human presence grew. The large trees were used to make masts for sailing ships, and because longleaf has such a high amount of resin, the trees were widely harvested to make waterproofing tars for the British mar-

itime industry. Feral hogs introduced by settlers damaged seedlings, and fire suppression damaged longleaf reproduction further. By the mid-nineteenth century only scattered remnants of
longleaf pine remained.

Brian van Eerden told me that he has been working with timber companies to reestablish longleaf habitat in southeast Virginia. Especially promising is a partnership between the state Department of Conservation and Recreation (DCR), the Nature
Conservancy, and International Paper Company, which owns a
large tract of pine habitat near Franklin called South Quay.

"The South Quay site has been a conservation priority for
years," said Brian. "Only a few areas are left in Virginia where you
can see native longleaf pine forest. The South Quay site is the best
we have. When it comes to rare habitats in North America, longleaf forests rank near the top of the list. Less than one percent of
the original range of longleaf pine remains in all of the southeastern United States."

The site is in southeast Virginia along the eastern side of the
Blackwater River and is part of the larger Chowan Sand Ridge, a
strip of land dominated by dry, sandy, rolling hills extending from
Gates County, North Carolina, to Isle of Wight County in Virginia.
The South Quay site encompasses several thousand acres and ex-
tends southward across the North Carolina line.

The special thing about longleaf pine is that the trees are the
keystone of an entire community of related plants and animals.
John Townsend of the Virginia Natural Heritage Program did a
botanical survey of South Quay that will help International Paper
draft a forestry management plan.

He said the South Quay tract is fascinating to botanists because
it has so many plants that are rare in Virginia. "South Quay represents the northern limit of many southern species," he said.
"Numerous plants at South Quay are found nowhere else in the
state."

Among the plants found at the tract are sandhills butterfly-
weed, sweet gallberry, pine-barren rush, northern sheep-laurel,

hairy seedbox, pyxie-moss, ciliate meadow-beauty, honey-cup, creeping blueberry, and fasciculate beakrush. South Quay is also the only known site in Virginia for the orange-bellied tiger beetle and the barrens dagger moth.

John Townsend's survey was the first since the famous Harvard University botanist Merritt Lyndon Fernald spent ten summers in the area in the 1930s and 1940s collecting and describing plant specimens. He collected orchids, carnivorous plants, and other plants that had never been seen before in Virginia.

"We found probably ninety percent of the plant species Fernald listed," said Townsend. "We even found a few he didn't have. The discouraging news is that one of his favorite collecting sites, which he described as a 'savannah-like swale,' is now under water. It was flooded when Union Camp built a holding pond years ago."

While generations of American school children have been taught to "prevent forest fires," conventional wisdom now is that fire is vital to the success of longleaf pine. Indeed, one of the reasons the forests disappeared years ago is because when towns and communities were built, settlers took fire suppression very seriously. Botanists are now using fire as a method of restoring longleaf pines and related plants to their native habitat. Lytton John Musselman, professor of botany at Old Dominion University, manages the Blackwater Ecologic Preserve in Isle of Wight County. He has been selectively burning portions of the preserve to remove dense underbrush and provide a foothold for a wide variety of plants and young trees. Without fire, he says, the longleaf pine cannot adequately reproduce and its descendants cannot be sustained.

Longleaf pine has adapted well to harsh conditions. It grows in sandy, nutrient-poor soils, and it has tough, thick bark that makes it fire-resistant. The tree depends upon fire for the nutrients and minerals that sustain life. Adult trees are protected by asbestos-like bark, and even the young buds are protected by a thick layer of needles. The shape of the tree also tends to direct fire upward, away from the buds of its seedlings. When the fire burns itself out, the ashes replenish the soil with nutrients and essential minerals.

Fire, then, feeds adult trees, clears the way for young ones, and reestablishes other plants whose seeds have been dormant, awaiting the right conditions.

As longleaf pines returned at Blackwater, so did other plants of the longleaf community, including mosses, pitcher plants, orchids, and others. More may still be dormant, banked in the soil, awaiting rebirth and baptism by fire.

NORTH CAROLINA

From Corolla to Calabash

THE CASUAL VISITOR TO THE NORTH CAROLINA COAST might easily come away with the impression that the Outer Banks will soon be covered with hotels, condominiums, and strip malls. It is true that the islands and barrier beaches of the Carolina coast have become some of the most popular tourist and retirement destinations in the East, and stretches of beach that once were wild are now stacked elbow-to-elbow with luxury condominiums and hotels.

But there still remains a wild side to the Carolina coast; it's just a little more difficult to find. I drove the entire coast, beginning in Corolla and ending in Calabash, just north of the South Carolina line, and I found places where you can still walk for miles on a deserted beach, paddle a canoe on a wilderness river, catch fish, hunt ducks, watch migrating birds, and hike trails that wind through old maritime forests.

If you drive down North Carolina Route 12 from Corolla, you'll find that the groves of oaks and cedars are now filled with luxury residences; the area has seen extensive development in the last ten years. But across Currituck Sound, life goes on as it has for centuries, with fishing and hunting still a part of the rural tradition of the area. In the northern part of Currituck Sound is Mackay Island National Wildlife Refuge, a magnet for waterfowl where conservation measures were begun in the 1930s by the founder of Ducks Unlimited.

The Southern Shores to Bodie Island corridor may be the most highly developed stretch along the Outer Banks, but even here are places where you can escape the rigors of the world for a day. Nags Head Woods is a maritime forest preserve of more than one thousand acres, just off the commercial strip. Farther south is Pea Island

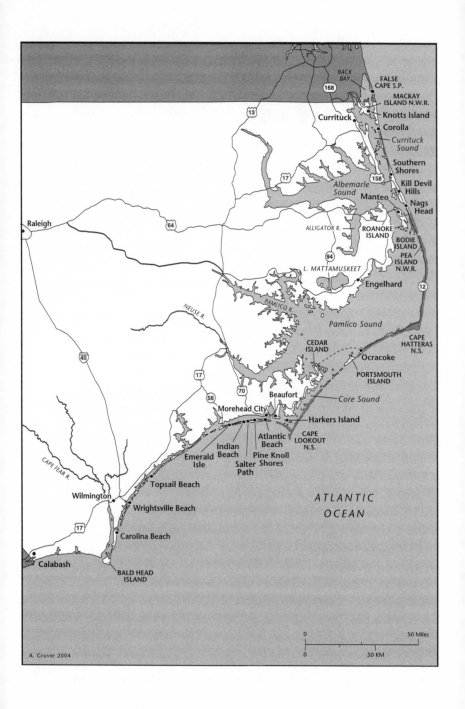

BACK
BAY
FALSE
CAPE S.P.
MACKAY
ISLAND N.W.R.
Knotts Island
Corolla
Currituck Sound
Southern Shores
Kill Devil Hills
Nags Head
BODIE ISLAND
PEA ISLAND N.W.R.
Currituck
Albemarle Sound
Manteo
ROANOKE ISLAND
ALLIGATOR R.
L. MATTAMUSKEET
Engelhard
Pamlico Sound
CAPE HATTERAS N.S.
PAMLICO R.
NEUSE R.
CEDAR ISLAND
Ocracoke
PORTSMOUTH ISLAND
Beaufort
Core Sound
Morehead City
Harkers Island
Indian Beach
Atlantic Beach
CAPE LOOKOUT N.S.
Emerald Isle
Salter Path
Pine Knoll Shores
Raleigh
Topsail Beach
CAPE FEAR R.
Wilmington
Wrightsville Beach
ATLANTIC OCEAN
Carolina Beach
Calabash
BALD HEAD ISLAND

0   50 Miles
0   50 KM

A. Gruver 2004

National Wildlife Refuge and Cape Hatteras National Seashore, a sanctuary of miles of wild beach. The protected waters around Roanoke Island are perfect for canoeing and kayaking, and if you drive west from Manteo and cross Croatan Sound, you'll find some real wilderness country in the Alligator River area. Farther south, Lake Mattamuskeet is a rural gem, a refuge that attracts hundreds of waterfowl each fall and winter.

I've found that one of the best ways to explore the Carolina coast is to hitch a ride on a ferry. North Carolina has an outstanding system of ferries that are one of the great bargains in public transportation. I crossed from Hatteras Island to Ocracoke on the ferry, and then drove through Cedar Island to Beaufort and Morehead City, crossing miles of salt marsh and tidal creeks.

Each of the coastal communities of the southern Outer Banks has its own personality. Atlantic Beach and Pine Knoll Shores have new hotels and expensive condominiums tucked back into the groves of live oak. Farther south, along Topsail Beach near Jacksonville, the beach houses are more eclectic, with a mix of traditional Outer Banks cottages, new construction, and parks filled with recreational vehicles. In the Wilmington area there is Wrightsville Beach, Carolina Beach, and Bald Head Island, but the draw here is the Cape Fear River, which begins as a wild blackwater stream far inland and empties into the Atlantic a few miles downstream from the historic city.

While the beach areas of the Carolina coast have seen extensive development in recent years, there still are many places to explore, many places to spend a day hiking or canoeing, many places to enjoy Carolina's wild side.

Currituck

Living the sporting life

Barbara and Wilson Snowden can stand on their front porch and look across five miles of open water and two ways of life. The Snowdens live in a rambling Victorian Italianate home built not long after the Civil War ended. It's high on the banks of Currituck Sound, just down the street from the ferry landing that connects Currituck with Knotts Island. In the distance is the Currituck Beach Lighthouse, the northernmost lighthouse on the Outer Banks. Just south of the light is the Whalehead Club, perhaps the most famous and lavish of the sportsmen's retreats built on the sound in the early 1900s.

When Wilson was growing up, the northern beaches were wild, with an unending panorama of dunes, beach, and salt marsh. Low-lying forests of live oak and cedar lined the upland, a green byway that ran along the spine of the narrow spit of land. Today, Route 12 runs along what might have been the dune line, two lanes of asphalt linking the northern beach with Southern Shores, Kill Devil Hills, Nags Head, and the mainland. Route 12 is never far from the water—the sound to the west, the ocean to the east—yet you can drive twenty miles north to the Currituck Beach Lighthouse and see no evidence of either sound or ocean unless a high tide has created a temporary puddle in the roadway.

Those live oak forests are filled with condos these days. There are stately private homes, fine shops, expensive restaurants, and beach stores that sell hammocks and things made of shells. Wilson Snowden used to hunt ducks here and fish in the surf for striped bass and bluefish. Local families would cross the sound on a Sunday afternoon after church and have a picnic lunch on the beach, and the children would play in the dunes. Duck blinds have been replaced by million-dollar homes on the northern beaches, and the

Whalehead Club is a museum, a memorial to what life was once like on these Outer Banks. At least they named the streets for ducks.

If you stand on the grounds of the Whalehead Club and look back toward Wilson and Barbara Snowden's home, you'll see the horizon as an uninterrupted green line. This is Currituck County as it was and is, separated from the Outer Banks by much more than open water. While visitors to the northern beaches enjoy the finer trappings of luxurious homes and restaurants, life on the mainland still revolves around more elemental matters: the land, the season, the weather, the water, the wildlife.

When I visited the Snowdens, Wilson was in a bit of a dilemma. He had the afternoon free. Should he go duck hunting or striped bass fishing? Scaup (a type of diving duck) were trading around the sound in ragged strings. A cold front was on the way and the birds were nervous, not staying in one place for long—good news for duck hunters. Wilson's gunning skiff was moored at the ferry dock. It was gassed up and ready to go. Yet, as Barbara pointed out, striped bass baked with potatoes and onions sure would be good for supper. I had the feeling Wilson was about to go fishing.

Wilson Snowden has caught bass and shot ducks on Currituck Sound for most of his fifty-nine years. His family's general store, a few feet from the house, was once a gathering place for the Currituck community. Back when it was legal to sell ducks, the Snowdens would pack canvasbacks, scaup, and black ducks in barrels, chill them with ice, and put them on schooners bound for Baltimore. The store is closed now, and when Wilson goes duck hunting, it has more to do with keeping a tradition alive than putting food on the table.

For Wilson Snowden, duck hunting today also has more to do with the hunt than with ducks. Seasons are shorter than they were when he was growing up, limits are modest, and game laws are strictly enforced. "If all people want to do is shoot, they're going to be disappointed," he says. "Duck hunting is all about the experience of being out there on the water in a blind, your decoys set, and having ducks come into your rig. Whether you kill a duck or not is secondary. It's the experience of the hunt that I love."

Whalehead Club is being restored as a historic site, part of
the Currituck Beach Lighthouse historic compound, and Wilson
would like to see a duck hunt become part of the interpretation of
life on Currituck Sound. "I'd love to have a blind there, set out
decoys, and be able to take people out there and just let them get
the feel for what it's like, without actually shooting ducks. Duck
hunting is not simply a sport, it's a major part of the history and
culture of this area. I'd like people to experience that firsthand."

Barbara Snowden moved to Currituck from the Charlotte area
in 1967 to teach school. She had no intention of living permanently
in Currituck, but then she met Wilson, they got married in 1970,
and she has become a student of Currituck County history. The
history of waterfowl hunting is especially appealing to her because
the Snowden family is directly involved. "I remember seeing an
old sign long ago in the store that had duck prices. Canvasbacks
would bring one price, scaup another, black ducks another. I wish
I had saved that sign."

Currituck was one of the four original counties in North Carolina and was given an Indian name meaning "land of the wild
goose," she says. Prior to the Civil War local people hunted ducks
to put food on the table, but after the war, during Reconstruction,
wealthy northerners began coming down to go hunting. The
wealthier hunters built clubs and lodges of their own, other clubs
operated on a membership basis, and some visitors simply boarded
with local families. In addition, before the Migratory Bird Treaty
Act of 1918 ended market gunning, ducks were sold to northern
restaurants by the thousands.

"Duck hunting was a major industry here, an important part of
the economy," says Barbara. "A large number of people worked for
the clubs as guides, decoy carvers, cooks, and maintenance workers. People took hunters into their homes. I think it broadened the
horizons of a lot of the people who lived here. It exposed them to
the world outside Currituck County."

And duck hunting is still a popular sport and tradition in Currituck. Drive the back roads and you'll see gunning skiffs parked in

driveways. They'll be painted in camouflage and will have decks covered with grass. Goose or duck decoys will be stacked in the bow.

A few miles south of the Snowdens, in a community called Poplar Branch, Tillman and Elsie Merrell live in a neatly kept bungalow. They have been married for seventy-one years. At age ninety-four, Tillman Merrell can tell you what duck hunting was like in Currituck Sound before the beach was covered by condos and upscale shops. When he was fourteen he began helping his father take out hunting parties, using a flock of live Canada geese as decoys. Tillman still looks like he could handle a gunning skiff and a rig of live decoys, but, he says, his knees are giving him some trouble. He gave up hunting two years ago.

Tillman keeps a large garden, still drives his pickup truck, and has an indelible memory when it comes to duck hunting on the sound. When he and his father hunted, it was a business, not a sport. Duck hunting brought cash to Currituck County, mainly from northern hunters who paid for lodging and meals, club memberships, guide services, and the preparation of the game they bagged.

"We kept a rig of twenty-five or thirty live Canada geese that we used as decoys," he says. "We'd take them out in the boat in coops, drive iron stobs into the bottom, and tether the geese to the stobs. My brother had a pet goose he named Bill, and Bill didn't have to be tethered. He'd swim around the flock, and if we saw a flock of geese coming, my brother would call to Bill, and Bill would begin honking and the geese would come right in. When we finished hunting, Bill would come back into the boat. He was tame, but he wouldn't let you touch him. He was fine as long as you didn't touch him."

* * *

The North Carolina ferry system is one of the great bargains of public transportation. Ferries connect many Outer Banks communities with the mainland, and in Currituck they get kids to and from school. The longer ferry rides, such as the two-and-a-half-hour crossing between Ocracoke and Cedar Island, cost about fifteen dollars, but many of the shorter rides are free.

I drove down the ramp at Currituck, was waved on board by an attendant dressed in khaki, and at precisely 11 A.M. the ferry backed away from the dock and headed northeast across Currituck Sound toward Knotts Island. The crossing takes about forty-five minutes, and there is no charge. Earlier, the ferry had transported a bus loaded with students from Knotts Island to Currituck to attend school. In a few hours, the return trip would be completed, but at midday there were only two vehicles on board—mine and a white pickup truck that belonged to the local public utility company.

A combination service station and fast-food franchise is just down the block from the ferry terminal, and on my way to catch the boat I picked up a large coffee and the local daily paper, the *Virginian-Pilot*. The forty-five-minute boat ride was just about right for both. By the time we reached Knotts Island the coffee was tepid and I had worked my way through the news, sports, entertainment, and comics, and was reading recipes for vegetarian chili in the food section.

My bike was in a rack on the back of the car, and I was looking forward to biking around Mackay Island National Wildlife Refuge. My legs were stiff from too much car time, and I was hyper from the coffee. I needed fresh air and exercise.

From the ferry terminal I turned left onto state Route 615 and headed north to Knotts Island, stopped at the Knotts Island Market for a tuna on wheat and a root beer, and was soon at the Mackay Island refuge. The land here is low and marshy, and the wildlife refuge surrounds the community of Knotts Island. The refuge occupies more than eight thousand acres and includes shoreline along Currituck Sound, Back Creek, Barleys Bay, and Back Bay in Virginia. The emphasis here is on birds, especially waterfowl, and if you want to paddle your canoe to look at them, there are twenty miles of boating trails. A hiking and biking trail begins near Route 615 and winds its way around freshwater impoundments westward to the sound, and then loops back to the starting point for a ride of about six miles. If you continue north-ward on Route 615, you'll soon find yourself in Virginia, passing through towns with such wonderful names as Creeds, Munden, Back Bay, Pungo, and Nimmo. Here, Route 615 becomes Princess Anne Road and leads on to the great residential subdivisions of Virginia Beach.

I was ready to ride, but first I stopped by the refuge visitor center to say hello to Peggy Vanzant, who works in the bar at the visitor center. Peggy was wearing brown Fish and Wildlife Service jeans, a matching short-sleeved shirt, and a headset, which was connected to a telephone that seemed a bit peevish. "Mackay Island National Wildlife Refuge," Peggy said repeatedly into the headset.

Peggy was not serving shots of Jack Daniels to refuge visitors on the morning I stopped by. Instead, she handed me a map, pointed out the bike route, and gave me a quick tour of the visitor center. It's a low-slung building with lots of dark woodwork, heavy furni-ture, stone fireplace, and stuffed birds and animals. The place drips with testosterone. Hunting lodge, I guessed.

"They had some great times here," Peggy says. "Hunted ducks all day and played poker all night. If these walls could talk . . ."

Peggy's office, on the left as you enter the building, used to be the bar. The gun room, which is now a restroom, was on the right. Past her office is a great room and a deck with a view. The dining hall was on the left, the bedrooms down a hallway on the right. The bedrooms are offices now, and the dining room is used for meetings.

The bike trails are a few miles south of the visitor center, a short distance from the Knott's Island Market. I parked the car next to a kiosk, looked at the map, picked up a brochure on birds, and pulled the bike out of the rack. The tuna-on-wheat and a root beer went into the bike bag, along with a bottle of water and a few Fig Newtons for dessert.

The bike trails here are multipurpose service roads, hard-packed clay and gravel wide enough for good-sized trucks. On most days, though, only pedestrians and bicyclists are allowed. I rode from the kiosk through a farm field, a pinewoods, and then to a marshy area and around a gate to East Pool, a shallow impoundment where waterfowl gather in great numbers in the winter. The trail continues west along the impoundment and then to some flooded hardwoods where wood ducks were feeding in the shallow water.

The trail makes a hard left where it meets Currituck Sound, and then it runs south along the water to Live Oak Point. There once was a mansion here, a stately old home overlooking the sound, and its owner was a conservationist who began some of the water control practices that were expanded when the wildlife refuge was created in 1960.

The mansion was owned by Joseph P. Knapp, a wealthy New York publisher who purchased the land in 1918 from the writer and preacher Thomas Dixon. Knapp experimented with various wildlife management techniques and in 1930 formed the "More Gamebirds in America" foundation, which later became the waterfowl conservation organization Ducks Unlimited (DU). Joseph Knapp held the first organizational meeting for DU in 1936, and the organization was incorporated in 1938.

Past the mansion site the trail leaves the sound and heads back east on the southern perimeter of the impoundment, completing the loop near the entrance gate. Although Knapp's mansion no longer exists, he has a fitting legacy in these impoundments and other techniques he helped develop to provide a winter home for waterfowl. From October through spring the skies here are clouded with flocks of snow geese, Canada geese, and other waterfowl. Mr. Knapp, no doubt, would be pleased at the sight.

* * *

The duck hunting clubs of Currituck County today elicit a wide range of emotions. Certainly, they are part of the history and culture of the area, but to look at old photographs of men posing with a hundred or more dead birds leads one to think that this was an era of excess, waste, and a disregard for wildlife.

While club members did kill many ducks and geese, some of the more forward-thinking landowners, such as Joseph Knapp, did the waterfowl population more good than harm. In 1900 there were no wildlife refuges, few private conservation organizations, and no groups like Ducks Unlimited, which today has protected tens of thousands of acres of land for wildlife. Conservation was the domain of the wealthy landowner, who could afford to purchase large tracts of land and manage it for wildlife instead of profit. The concept of wildlife conservation as a function of the federal government is relatively new.

Writing in *Wildfowl Art Journal*, a publication of the Ward Museum of Wildfowl Art in Salisbury, Maryland, Samuel H. Dyke argues that gunning clubs were the prototypes of conservation organizations we have today. "Several clubs raised and released more ducks than they shot each season," writes Dyke. "Sanctuary ponds for resting and feeding were designated on club property, and even the controversial practice of baiting is credited with sustaining the waterfowl during freeze-ups. Ownership of large tracts of wetlands by these clubs saved these fragile areas from commercial exploitation until they could be acquired by public and private conservation organizations."

Archie Johnson and Bud Coppedge, writing in *Gun Clubs and Decoys of Back Bay and Currituck Sound* (Virginia Beach: CurBac Press, 1991), say that between the 1870s and 1920s there were more than one hundred gunning clubs and lodges in a one-hundred-mile stretch along Back Bay and Currituck Sound.

One of the most famous of the private clubs was the Ragged Island Club, which was in Back Bay, just over the Virginia line. The club was chartered by nine Norfolk businessmen in 1891 as the Ragged Island Gunning Association of Virginia. The club property consisted of about four thousand acres in a cluster of thirty-two marshy islands west of what now is False Cape State Park. A two-story clubhouse was built on the largest island, and it was well appointed with a parlor, dining room, wine cellar, and bedrooms for the members. A dwelling for the caretaker's family was separated from the main building. The club survived until 1939, when the property was sold to the federal government and became part of Back Bay National Wildlife Refuge.

Life in the gunning clubs was well documented by Alexander Hunter, a northern Virginia writer who was a member of the Ragged Island Club. In *The Huntsman in the South* (New York: Neale, 1908) Hunter wrote of a visit by President Benjamin Harrison. Harrison arrived at the club accompanied only by a valet and spent four days duck hunting. Unlike today, there was no Secret Service, no press corps, no advisors. Indeed, the president was out of touch with Washington for the entire time, as the club had no telephone or telegraph.

The president was an excellent shot, Hunter reported, and helped stock the club kitchen with numerous canvasback ducks during his visit. While at the club he was treated as just another member, not president of the United States. On the final day of his hunt, however, Harrison gave the club members cause to worry. It was a windy February day, with snow and sleet flying, and the president left alone for his blind before dawn. Other club members fanned out across the four thousand acres to blinds of their own, and by mid-afternoon most had returned to the lodge, cold and hungry. Cocktail time came, it grew dark, and soon the cook announced that dinner was served. President Harrison was nowhere to be found, and the club members became worried.

"It would be a terrible reflection on them if anything should happen to [the president]," Hunter wrote with obvious irony. "Every man seized a lantern and started across the swamp, and it was well that we did so, for the President had missed the footbridge and was wading slowly and laboriously through the black ooze of the swamp toward the clubhouse. He was already up to his hips and very tired; almost exhausted, in fact."

Hunter wrote that Currituck Sound had the largest concentration of hunting lodges of any area in the world: "Currituck Sound is interspersed with many islands and marshes . . . and there is not a foot of this ground that is not owned . . . and watched over as if it sheltered a gold mine. All the best points have been bought by syndicates, and the members of these have formed clubs. As a consequence, a small area on the North Carolina coast contains the largest collection of clubhouses in so small a space to be found anywhere in the world. A strip about forty miles long by three to ten miles wide is literally sown with them, ranging from the shanty of the market gunner to the spacious mansion."

If Hunter could visit the northern beaches of the Outer Banks today, he would likely not recognize the place. He wrote in "The Sportsmen's Clubs of Currituck" that "the strip of sand that separates the Atlantic Ocean from Currituck Sound is the very embodiment of desolation."

But Hunter seemed to have had a grudging admiration for the local people. "The men are as tough as pine knots," he wrote. "They have sallow skins that are thick as parchment, and loose, raw-boned figures. They earn their living entirely by fishing, hunting, and acting as guides; at home they are lazy as Indians. These eastern North Carolinians are born sportsmen. Expertness with the gun, like their poverty, is their heritage; and they, in the vernacular of the coast, 'shoot to kill.'"

The Outer Banks and Beyond

History and nature intermingle

Over the crashing of the waves, over the roar of the wind, I sometimes think I can hear them. On an early morning I walked the beach at Pea Island National Wildlife Refuge near Cape Hatteras. Men died in storms off these shoals. Others were rescued by the heroic action of coastguardsmen.

When the wind howls and the surf kicks up, I can imagine what it must have been like. Sails tattered, planks torn apart, a ship is blown aground, dragging keel. Then the persistent waves break on deck, the hold floods, the ship lists, and the crew prepares to abandon ship.

If they were lucky, their predicament would have been noticed by lookouts at the Pea Island Lifesaving Station. These men would have driven a team with lifesaving equipment through the gale, a breeches buoy would have been launched from the berm of the beach to the stricken ship, and one by one the crew would have been plucked off and taken to safety.

Over the centuries, many have been so lucky, others have not. Hiking the beach here in a winter storm, I can imagine what it might have been like for seasick crewmen, near panic, for rescuers who put their lives on the line in the worst of conditions. I can hear their shouts over the din of breaking surf.

Driving south on state Route 12 through the Outer Banks, I passed restaurants and hotels and condominiums, and then entered Pea Island NWR and stepped back in time. The building boom of the Outer Banks stops at Oregon Inlet, with miles of wild beach protected as Cape Hatteras National Seashore.

Pea Island National Wildlife Refuge is at the northern limits of the protected area, with about 13 miles of undeveloped beach, 6,000

acres of upland, and 25,700 acres of boundary water on the Pamlico Sound, where hunting is off-limits. At Pea Island, you can tell
when the seasons change by watching the birds. Sometime in early
March the ring-billed gulls depart, heading north to raise a family,
and they are replaced by laughing gulls, which have come here from
points south, also to raise a family.

On the coast, the appearance of laughing gulls marks the beginning of spring, and they arrive each year with amazing punctual-
ity. I note in my field guide each year the first sighting of laughing
gulls, and the date seldom varies by more than a week. We saw our
first on an early March trip to Pea Island, and about a week later
they showed up at our home on Virginia's Eastern Shore, gathering noisily on the boat dock as they went about their courtship.
They will nest in a salt marsh out near the Chesapeake Bay.

Lynn, Tom, and I usually plan an early spring trip to the Outer
Banks to get an early look at laughing gulls and other spring birds,
and Pea Island is usually the place to go. Like many coastal wildlife
refuges, Pea Island was created in the late 1930s to provide a migration stop and overwintering area for waterfowl. Freshwater
impoundments were built between the dune line and Pamlico
Sound, and the migrating birds quickly find it.

The dikes that created the impoundment were built by the Civilian Conservation Corps in 1938 and have been enlarged and widened
over the years. Today they make up one of the most unusual hiking trails along the coast. Hiking the entire circuit requires a walk
of about four miles, but it's worth it. Depending upon the season,
the impoundments will have tundra swans, geese, a wide variety of
ducks, shorebirds, and resident wading birds such as great blue
herons and egrets. A refuge publication says 265 different species
of birds have been spotted here.

We began a recent hike of Pea Island with a walk on the beach,
near the spot where the Pea Island Lifesaving Station once stood.
This is the only station in America to have been manned exclu-
sively by African Americans, and although the station is now gone,
a kiosk marks the spot. In addition, photographs and artifacts are
on display at the North Carolina Aquarium in Manteo.

We then drove to the visitor center on the west side of Route 12 and said "good morning" to Mary Vansickle, who not long ago logged her three-thousandth hour as a Pea Island refuge volunteer. The visitor center is small, but a large window provides a great view of the impoundment. Mary pointed out a pair of ospreys, recent spring arrivals, which were building a nest on a platform erected in the pond.

"This is a unique place," she said. "We have the shallow ponds here in the refuge, the tidal waters of Pamlico Sound, and the dunes and ocean just east of us. So we get a wide variety of wildlife. Ospreys nest here in the pond and on the sound, and in summer sea turtles will come ashore and nest on the ocean beach."

Mary pointed out the entrance to the hiking trail, so we gathered the binoculars and the field guide and stashed some bottled water and snacks in our jacket pockets. The trail begins just south

Bird-watching at Pea Island

of the visitor center, and the first section runs through a grove of live oaks, which turn the path into a leafy tunnel. The trailhead is flanked by small ponds, and when we visited, the turtles were sunning themselves on every available log.

The trail soon opens to offer a great view of North Pond, and an elevated viewing platform provides a look at this impoundment as well as New Field Pond, south of the trail. The ponds here are very shallow, so they attract dabbling ducks such as blacks, pintails, gadwalls, mallards, and shovelers, all of which were present in great numbers, as were tundra swans, snow geese, Canada geese, and waders such as white ibises, herons, and egrets.

A second observation platform is at the southwest corner of the trail, and it provides a great view of the impoundments. This platform is a good turn-around point if you want a short hike of about a mile, or you can head north on the service road that runs atop the dike. This will take you along the western perimeter of the pond, and finally back to Route 12.

Pea Island NWR provides sanctuary for a great variety of songbirds and waterfowl, and it is one of those places where the human imprint seems to have bonded. Although the Pea Island Lifesaving Station is gone, you can walk these beaches and the dike trail, look beyond the crashing surf, and imagine what life might have been like for those in peril, and for those whose mission was to snatch them from danger.

※　※　※

If you drive north from Pea Island, turn left onto U.S. Route 64 and cross the bridge over Roanoke Sound, you'll find yourself in Manteo, one of the most spectacular small towns in North Carolina. The town is squeaky clean, with inviting restaurants and shops, a spacious waterfront, and popular attractions such as the North Carolina Aquarium, the Elizabethan Gardens, and Roanoke Island Festival Park. The popular play "The Lost Colony" is presented here during the summer, telling the dramatic story of early settlers who built a community on Roanoke Island and then mysteriously disappeared.

Roanoke Island is a handsome bit of real estate, separated from the Outer Banks by Roanoke Sound, and from the mainland by Croatan Sound. So it draws its share of summer tourists from the beaches, but it still retains its hometown appeal. Manteo, the largest town on Roanoke Island, has been a port town for centuries, as a visit to the festival park will attest. While downtown Manteo has its appeal, the best way to see the town, and Roanoke Island, is by boat. And so I called Tom Fotti, who works for Kitty Hawk Sports, and we made arrangements to take a look at Roanoke by kayak.

Tom and I got together on an early spring afternoon during the week, and we had the waters of Roanoke Sound to ourselves. We put in at the public launch in Manteo near Festival Park, and as we paddled past replicas of early sailing ships the irony of the situation struck me. Here we were in one of the first places in America to be explored by European settlers, and we were in boats very much like those used by the first explorers, and by the Native Americans before them. There were, of course, differences. Their boats would have been made of wood or animal skin. Ours were made of roto-molded polyethylene—plastic, in other words. But our little boats took us confidently and swiftly along the beaches and marshes, and we explored tiny creeks that motorboats would never have attempted.

As soon as Tom and I were out of the harbor it was like stepping back in time. Roanoke Island is rich in history. The first English child in the New World, Virginia Dare, was born here at Fort Raleigh on August 18, 1587. Virginia Dare was a member of "The Lost Colony," whose disappearance is still a mystery, made popular by the play written by Paul Greene.

We paddled alongside the *Elizabeth II,* berthed at Roanoke Island Festival Park, and then headed north along the eastern edge of the island. Tom majored in engineering at Clemson University but has shunned the corporate world in order to do something he truly loves: paddling small boats.

"I got lucky," he said. "I've got a job that I truly do enjoy, and this is the perfect place to do it. I really enjoy the lifestyle of the Outer Banks. My fiancée works at the North Carolina Aquarium, and she loves the beach and the ocean, so this is where we want to be."

Tom says the popularity of sea kayaking has grown tremendously on the Outer Banks in the past few years. "I got interested in whitewater kayaking growing up in New Jersey," he said, "but down here I've made a natural transition to kayak touring. There are so many opportunities here."

Tom and I left the sound and entered a narrow canal. Black needlerush grew along both sides, and Fotti told me that Native Americans of the area used the sharp points of the plant with dyes to tattoo themselves. The canal, probably dug during the 1930s to drain the marshland, opened into a small creek that wound through a brackish marsh. A great blue heron patrolled the shallows, searching for small fish.

"The kayak is a perfect fit for this area," he said. "It draws about four inches of water, so you can get to places that motorboats can't reach. It's the perfect platform for fishing, watching birds, or just touring. And it's environmentally clean. It doesn't pollute, doesn't make noise, and it can be recycled."

The boats we were paddling were Perception Carolinas, about fifteen feet long, equipped with foot-controlled rudders we didn't bother to use on a still day with little current running. Longer kayaks with watertight compartments are used for open water or for extended trips, but these seemed just about right for the waters around Roanoke Island. Stable, a bit beamy, but maneuverable enough to make it possible to explore narrow and winding creeks that meander through the marsh.

"What we have here is a combination of sheltered water and an abundance of wildlife," said Tom. "On our group trips, we pretty much stay in flat water. Paddling in the Kitty Hawk Woods area is one of our most popular trips. My personal favorite is the Pea Island area, where there are thousands of birds from fall into spring. Plus the area has so much history, so much folklore."

Tom and I returned to the Manteo boat ramp as the sun was getting low. He mentioned that he needed to get back to the store and finish packing. He was leaving the next day to help guide a group of college students on a trip to the Florida Everglades. "It's a job," he said laughing. "Well, it's a job and it's fun."

* * *

Drive down U.S. Route 158 through Nags Head and Kill Devil Hills, and you might get the idea that all the sand on this narrow beach has been covered with condos and strip malls. Pause for a moment and listen for the ocean. What is this we hear, pneumatic hammers and the clatter of plywood sheathing going up?

But when you get near milepost 9, look for a sign that says Ocean Acres Drive. There also will be a nondescript brown sign that says simply "The Nature Conservancy." Turn west here, drive through the residential area until the paved road ends, and continue on the dirt road for another quarter mile. On your left will be a pair of rustic buildings that are the headquarters of Nags Head Woods Ecological Preserve. Pull into the parking lot and begin to experience Nags Head as it was before the word "condo" entered the lexicon.

Given the rapid development of the northern Outer Banks in the last ten years, this is a remarkable natural area. It offers more than one thousand acres of pristine maritime forest and dunes in the center of a resort area where every square foot of sand is coveted by developers. That it has survived intact, and indeed has grown in recent years, is the result of work by a number of organizations, including the Nature Conservancy, the towns of Nags Head and Kill Devil Hills, Friends of Nags Head Woods, and concerned individuals who have generously donated land.

I parked my car on a recent weekday, hiked the trails for nearly two hours, and had the place to myself. The small visitor center is a good place to start when exploring Nags Head Woods. There you can pick up a trail map and brochures on each of the six trails in the preserve, as well as other information.

I began my hike on one of the easier trails, Center Trail, a modest loop that begins and ends at the visitor center. The trail is short, but it covers diverse habitat, winding along old forested dunes, and then descending to swales crossed by wooden bridges. If you have limited time, this will give you a nice introduction to the natural life of a maritime forest.

I had a bit more time to spend, so I walked back out Ocean Acres Drive to a split rail fence that marks the beginning of the Discovery Trail, a loop of about a half mile that winds through a forest of pine, sweet gum, and red bay. About halfway around the loop, a side trail leads to Roanoke Trail, which goes westward through the forest and down to the waters of Roanoke Sound.

Roanoke Trail not only provides a scenic walk, but it also gives visitors a glimpse of what life might have been like here a century or more ago. I passed a small cemetery, the resting place of the Tillett family, who lived here until the 1940s. Some of the markers, weathered by time, date back to the mid-1800s.

Roanoke Trail is what would have served as the Tillett family's driveway in 1900, intersecting with Old Nags Head Road, which linked that community with Kill Devil Hills. About halfway down the trail, on the left side, I found a pile of brick rubble and some foundation blocks, all that remains of the Tilletts' farmstead. Cedar posts mark what's left of an old outbuilding, the bottom of which had been dug out, perhaps for the storage of vegetables.

Roanoke Trail crosses a bridge and ends at the edge of Roanoke Sound, where an ancient live oak, estimated to be five hundred years old, wears an iron spike believed to have been used by the Tilletts for processing game.

It is interesting to imagine what life might have been like for the Tilletts in 1900. They would have depended upon the sound for their livelihood, catching fish and shellfish spring through fall, shooting waterfowl in winter. They likely kept a small kitchen garden near the homeplace.

Like many islands along the North Carolina and Virginia coast, this one had a substantial human population a century or more ago. The Nags Head community is said to have had sufficient people to support two churches, a school, and a store. Farther north, just above the Virginia line, Wash Woods in False Cape State Park had a similar community. Hog Island, on the Eastern Shore, had a village called Broadwater, where more than two hundred people lived. All are long gone.

The important thing about what Nags Head Woods Preserve has to offer is that not only can we learn what the trees, plants, birds and animals are like in a maritime forest, but we can also hike the trails, find small mementos from earlier people, and use our imaginations to see what their lives might have been like.

I imagine they lived simply but well, depending upon the waters and marshes of Roanoke Sound to sustain their lives. It is remarkable how our lives and expectations change over just a few generations. I had a hotel room waiting for me on the beach a short drive away. I was looking forward to a dip in the pool and a soak in the hot tub before going to the dining room for dinner. I wonder what the Tilletts would have thought about that.

* * *

It was swan weather. The temperature was around forty, the air was still, and a light rain was falling. Clouds hung over Lake Mattamuskeet, which was gray and flat as sheet metal. I could hear swans but couldn't see them. They were up there, somewhere.

The tundra swan has a beautiful voice, feminine and fragile for a bird so large. It is a high-pitched voice, somewhat tentative, as if afraid to interrupt. If you want to see tundra swans, Lake Mattamuskeet is the place to go, and don't worry about the clouds. They'll blow over.

The lake is in rural Hyde County. I drove from Manteo across the Croatan Sound bridge and then headed south on U.S. Route 264, which goes through Alligator River National Wildlife Refuge and then to Englehard, where I booked a room in the Engelhard Hotel, a modest frame building you reach by driving across a wooden bridge that spans a canal. Engelhard is the largest town in the Lake Mattamuskeet area, and it's popular among fishermen who come to try their luck in Pamlico Sound. It's also a working watermen's town, and the docks along the waterfront are filled with packinghouses where seafood is off-loaded from fishing boats and shipped to market.

Lake Mattamuskeet is on the Albemarle-Pamlico Peninsula in what is known as pocosin country. Pocosin is a Native American term meaning, literally, "swamp on a hill," and the area is dotted with pocosin lakes, swamps, and former swamps that were long ago converted to farm fields. The land is flat, and fields stretch for miles, like a swampy Great Plain. The soil is black and rich and packed with organic matter. I'd love to bring some home for my garden.

This fertile peninsula, separated by only a few miles of open water from the barrier beaches of the coast, is the antithesis of the Outer Banks. There are historic farmsteads, small communities, churches, country stores, and a pervading sense of quiet. Hyde County has 634 square miles and only 6,000 residents, so open space prevails. The county has several villages, but there are no incorporated towns and no town taxes. Much of the land here is protected as national wildlife refuge. Alligator River NWR has more than 150,000 acres. Pocosin Lakes NWR, northwest of Lake Mattamuskeet, encompasses 110,000 acres and has an extensive system of canoe trails, allowing visitors the opportunity to see everything from warblers to red wolves. The area has the largest concentration of black bears in the southeast, and it is at the northern range of many species associated with southern habitat—for example, alligators and anhingas (a fish-eating bird related to the cormorant). So when it comes to North Carolina's wild coast, it doesn't get much wilder than Hyde County.

Mattamuskeet National Wildlife Refuge is unusual in that it consists mainly of water. It was created in 1934, ending periodic attempts to drain the shallow, forty-thousand-acre lake. Mattamuskeet now provides a temporary home for thousands of migratory birds, chiefly waterfowl, as well as recreational opportunities for visitors.

The wildlife refuge includes the lake and a fringe of land surrounding it. It begins near the town of Fairfield, where Route 94 crosses the lake, offering great views in all directions. Tundra swans can frequently be seen along this drive, and you can pull off at an observation platform on the east side of the causeway to get a better look.

The refuge entrance is on the left just as you cross the lake, and the drive to the refuge office provides a good opportunity to see swans and other waterfowl. On the right side of the entrance road is a shallow impoundment, which, when I visited, had swans, coots, gadwalls, pintails, black ducks, mallards, and other waterfowl.

The most unusual feature of the refuge is Mattamuskeet Lodge, a huge building of white brick and red tile roof, built over a canal just beyond the refuge office. The lodge was built in 1915 to house the world's largest pumping station, part of a plan to drain Lake Mattamuskeet and the surrounding swampland.

Lake Mattamuskeet Lodge

Inspired by a similar project in Holland, a group of business-men envisioned draining the lake and swamp and creating a "model community" of farms and residences. After several attempts by various groups, the plan was abandoned, and in 1934 the property was sold to the federal government, leading to the creation of Mattamuskeet Migratory Bird Refuge.

Civilian Conservation Corps members went to work on the refuge, and the old pumping station was converted to a hunting and fishing lodge, with the huge smokestack becoming a 112-foot observation tower. The lodge was in operation until 1974 and was later listed on the National Register of Historic Places. Although the building has fallen into disrepair, a community group hopes to restore the property and use it for educational and interpretive activities.

A wildlife drive begins behind the lodge and runs about three miles alongside a canal and through a lakeside swamp. There are few open lake vistas along the drive. But the forested areas are good places to find migrating warblers during the spring migration.

If you want to see waterfowl, probably the best place on the refuge is Lake Landing, where a series of water control structures built around farmland attract tens of thousands of birds. Exploring this area calls for some walking, but it is well worth the effort.

Lake Landing is just off Route 94, about seven miles east of the refuge headquarters. There is a small parking area, and dike roads extend for several miles around impoundments that are planted in corn and other grain crops and then flooded. On a recent visit I saw thousands of snow geese and tundra swans, huge flocks of pintail ducks, coots, and numerous other waterfowl and wading birds.

Overlooking the lake, with swans and snow geese flying overhead, it's difficult to imagine that years ago people took in this same scene, but in place of open water they envisioned towns, residences, farms, and businesses. I have to admire the ambitions and dreams of people like that. But sometimes things work out for the best, despite our greatest intentions.

The Crystal Coast

Afoot and afloat in Carteret's jewel

With a southwest wind there were whitecaps on Pamlico Sound, but the *Silver Lake* ran smooth and true, the big diesels down below creating a soft rumble that rippled the surface of my coffee.

I had decided to take a winter cruise, one where I could get close to wildlife, hike a deserted ocean beach, and just sit back and watch the waves roll by. I'm not exactly a big spender, but I was willing to dig deep for such a winter break. I might even be tempted to part with, let's say, fifteen dollars.

That's what the toll taker asked for when I pulled into line at the ferry terminal in Ocracoke, although I admit to being a little put out because in the ferry brochure the fare was listed as ten dollars. "Went up August first," the toll taker explained.

I had already ridden the ferry from Hatteras to Ocracoke, which was free, so I suppose I couldn't complain about an extra five dollars to get my car and me from Ocracoke to Cedar Island.

At fifteen dollars the cruise from Ocracoke to Cedar Island is still a bargain. By way of comparison, the Cape May–Lewes Ferry on Delaware Bay costs twenty-five dollars for car and driver, plus eight dollars per passenger. The cruising time, two hours and fifteen minutes, is about the same, and while the Delaware Bay ferries are larger, the Carolina boats still provide a very comfortable cruise.

I was exploring the Outer Banks and wanted to see the southern beaches, and the most pleasurable way to get there is by boat. North Carolina happens to have a great public ferry system. The boats are clean, well maintained, and they travel on time. So it's a pleasure to park the car on the lower deck, climb the stairs to the passenger lounge, and watch through the windows as the cormorants fly by.

Winter is the perfect time to combine a boat trip and a beach hike. Traffic is light, the boats are uncrowded, and the sounds are filled with seabirds. Cormorants flew alongside in flocks of hundreds, and gulls circled over schools of rockfish. For much of the way, dolphins gracefully surfaced and dove just off our bow.

Most of Ocracoke Island is protected as national seashore, with about twelve miles of wild beach to explore. A short distance from the ferry landing, the road looks like a small airstrip: flat, wide, and straight. I drove for a few miles, passed a pony corral on the right, then parked the car and headed for the beach. I had packed a peanut butter and fig preserve sandwich and a bottle of water, so I picked up the binoculars and set off.

The dunes on the southern end of the island are low, covered with beach grass and shrubby cedars pruned by the salt wind. The berm is not wide, but there is plenty of room for walking. I picked up shells, watched brown pelicans dive beyond the breakers, and then found a sheltered spot in the dunes to have my sandwich. I didn't see another person.

The village of Ocracoke takes up most of the southern tip of the island. It's one of those great unspoiled beach towns that survived the sixties intact and went against the tide of upscale shops, fast food, and traffic lights. I parked the car and walked around the town, explored a few interesting shops, and took a side street to the Ocracoke Lighthouse, which was decorated for Christmas, a large wreath hanging from the light.

Ocracoke is one of those places you visit for an hour and want to stay for two days. But the ferry for Cedar Island was leaving soon, and I needed to be on it.

The boat was about half full. I parked on the lower deck, walked up to the passenger lounge, and stretched out with a cup of coffee at a table overlooking the bow. It felt good to sit down and relax after walking on the beach and exploring the town. Old ferries have a wonderful, welcoming feel about them, like a small-town diner. Everything is plastic and chrome and Formica. A coffee maker is lashed to a shelf, Styrofoam cups stacked nearby. It's a dollar a cup, honor system. Put your bill in the can with the slotted top.

I like the reassuring sound of the diesel engines deep in the belly of the ship. The *Silver Lake* has two, each producing 805 horsepower. They seem relaxed, unhurried, going about their business without fluster or bother. They'll have us in Cedar Island in two hours and a quarter.

The channel twists out of the Ocracoke harbor like a corkscrew, with red and green channel markers showing the position of numerous shoals. Some shoals even clear the water at low tide, creating temporary beaches, and they attract dozens of birds— various gulls, pelicans, and cormorants.

We soon entered open water and set a course for Cedar Island, which appeared as a narrow green line after we had been sailing for a little over an hour. I walked to the stern, stood on the rear deck, and looked back at Ocracoke. Very slowly it faded from view and then disappeared altogether.

※　※　※

Cedar Island, unlike the Outer Banks, is unhurried and unchanged. While thousands of tourists and retirees have headed for the beaches and their amenities, Cedar Island has had no such building boom. It's an inner island, with no ocean beach, but with some magnificent views of Pamlico Sound. State Route 12 runs from the ferry terminal through pinewoods and farm fields, and through Cedar Island National Wildlife Refuge, which occupies the northern tip of Carteret County. I turned left onto a narrow paved road and followed the shoreline of Cedar Island. A few weekend cottages were scattered along the waterfront, but most were modest getaways, unlike the hotels and condominiums on the oceanfront. This is a landscape of pine forest and salt marsh, and most of it is protected as wildlife refuge.

Route 12 winds its way through rural Carteret County toward Beaufort and Morehead City. It's a spectacular drive in any season, but especially in fall and winter when the *spartina* grasses are turning gold and black ducks scatter across the marsh, their underwings nearly white when illuminated by the low sun. I parked the car on the shoulder and walked along the marsh, breathing in that rich, salty aroma of low tide. Somewhere in the distance a black duck called, and then another. A great blue heron stalked a killifish at the edge of a shallow pond, moving very gracefully, catlike, until it struck with unexpected swiftness, and I could see the fish shining in its beak, squirming. The heron shook its head from side to side, flipped the fish and downed it, paused for a few seconds, and then resumed the hunt.

I realized that this scene has been playing out here for centuries: ducks, herons, fish, and a few humans living in close proximity, their lives enmeshed, part of the same landscape. I drove through communities that were edged right up to Core Sound—Lola, Atlantic, Sea Level, Smyrna, Harkers Island. Many of the families have lived here for generations. Some lived across the sound, on Portsmouth Island, Core Banks, Shackleford Banks. When those barrier beaches were higher, when sea level was lower, there were thriving communities, and with them arose a history and culture unique to this part of the coast.

As in Currituck County farther north, the sounds, the marshes, and the ocean have played a prominent role in the lives of the people who live here. Wildfowl hunting was a major factor, especially in winter, when wild ducks and geese supplemented a diet of fish and shellfish. In Harkers Island I stopped at the Core Sound Waterfowl Museum and examined some of the hunting decoys used in the area in the late 1800s and early 1900s. Decoy making is an ancient art here, one that combines form and function in the best possible way. Decoys were a tool to lure ducks, but the makers added their own vision and style. Collectors can readily distinguish black ducks made by different carvers.

It is said that the waterfowling traditions of Core Sound precede European settlement, that the Coree Indians, who were wise in the ways of wildfowl, taught the early settlers how to stalk, capture, and cook ducks and geese. These traditions are highly valued and have evolved through the years. While plastic decoys long ago replaced wooden ones in modern hunting rigs, the tradition of decoy making lives on, with many contemporary carvers applying modern techniques to this ancient art. Many examples are shown in the 20,000-square-foot waterfowl museum, and thousands of visitors come to Harkers Island each December for the annual Waterfowl Weekend to pay tribute to the history and culture of life on the sound, especially as it is interpreted through wildfowl art.

While the northern barrier beaches have seen unprecedented development in the last decade, more people lived on Portsmouth Island, Core Banks, and Shackleford Banks in the nineteenth century than now. The three islands are part of Cape Lookout National Seashore, which joined the national park system in March 1966. So what we have today are fifty-six miles of undeveloped coastal barrier beach, a wild landscape where one can walk along the breaking surf for hours and not see another soul. The islands are accessible only by ferry and private boat, which often makes them beyond the realm of the casual visitor and, therefore, special.

Although there are no longer permanent residents on the islands, reminders of the human presence are clearly seen. Perhaps the most unique is on Shackleford Banks, where a herd of more than one hundred wild horses roam the nine-mile-long island. The horses are descendents of Spanish mustangs introduced to the island by early European settlers more than four hundred years ago. These feral horses—once domestic and now wild—roam the island freely. In the west, horses like these are called mustangs.

The most visible reminder of the human presence on the banks is the Cape Lookout Lighthouse, which, in its various forms, has been an aid to mariners since 1812. The distinctive black and white "diagonal checkerboard" pattern of the Cape Lookout light distinguishes it from all the others, and it is part of America's maritime history. It has warned sailors of the dangerous shoals of the banks, it has guided ships to safe port, and it has tickled the imagination of visitors, who look at the light and wonder what life might have been like back in the Civil War era, when the lighthouse was one of the newest on the coast.

The first lighthouse at Cape Lookout was completed in 1812 and was a brick tower enclosed by a wood frame building painted with red and white stripes. Mariners complained that the tower was too short, and in 1852 plans were made for a new lighthouse as part of a coastal safety program under the United States Lighthouse Service. Construction began in 1857, and the new lighthouse opened two years later. The red brick tower became the prototype of all lighthouses on the Outer Banks, and it was not until 1873 that it was given the diagonal checkerboard pattern it wears today. The keeper's quarters, now the visitor center, were also built in 1873. A lighthouse keeper was stationed on the island until 1950, when the light was automated.

The mid-Atlantic region has had numerous island villages and settlements that are part of coastal history. Several of the barrier islands of Virginia had communities, mainly consisting of people tending to domestic animals pastured on the islands. A few of the communities grew to become substantial villages. The village of Broadwater on Hog Island had about 250 residents in the late 1800s. False Cape, on the Virginia–North Carolina line, had a church, school, and stores. At Cape Lookout National Seashore, the village of Portsmouth was a thriving town on the northern portion of the barrier chain on Ocracoke Inlet. The last residents of Portsmouth moved to the mainland many years ago, but the buildings that remain provide visitors with a vivid reminder of what life was like here more than a century ago.

Portsmouth Village was created by the North Carolina Assembly in 1753, and by 1770 it had grown to become one of the largest settlements on the Outer Banks. Portsmouth thrived because of its location on Ocracoke Inlet, which was a major trade route to North Carolina ports. But the inlet was shallow, and large ships found it difficult to navigate. Instead, they stopped at Portsmouth and transferred their cargo to lighter, shallow draft boats. Portsmouth became known as a lightering station, and storage, shipping, and residential facilities grew around the lightering business. The 1860 census reported that Portsmouth had 685 residents.

The decline of Portsmouth came with the Civil War. As the Union Army advanced down the Outer Banks, residents fled to the mainland. Many did not return after the war. Those who did found that Ocracoke Inlet had become even shallower, and most shippers began using a deeper inlet farther north. Fishing became the primary occupation for the islanders, and in 1894 a U.S. Lifesaving Station was opened, which played a vital role in the community for fifty years.

When the Lifesaving Service withdrew, Portsmouth declined, and by 1956 only seventeen residents remained. The last two residents, Elma Dixon and Marion Babb, reluctantly moved to the mainland in 1971.

Today, Portsmouth has a new life under the national seashore. The 250-acre historic district has been listed on the National Register of Historic Places, and visitors can walk the lanes of the village, see the modest homes of the community, and begin to understand what life might have been like on a barrier island a century ago.

*   *   *

Route 12 joins Route 70, which winds its way through rural Carteret County and then enters Beaufort (pronounced BO-furt), whose old downtown is snuggled up against the waterfront. Beaufort once was a hard-working watermen's town, and still is to some extent, but the downtown shops are more likely to sell antiques and art rather than ship supplies. A local outfitter operates a stable of sea kayaks out of the harbor, reflecting a growing interest in nature tourism, and across the street is the North Carolina Maritime Museum, which nicely captures the seafaring traditions of the region.

Across the Newport River from Beaufort is Morehead City, another old waterfront town that is expanding westward along Route 70 in an ever-widening landscape of strip malls, restaurant chains, and car dealerships. The heart of the city, though, is the old downtown, where the railroad track runs along the highway median. The waterfront is just off the main drag, and there are numerous shops with local art and restaurants where the seafood is so fresh it was part of the saltwater ecosystem just prior to being cooked.

The Sanitary Fish Market and Restaurant is a local landmark noted for its well-polished pine woodwork, a sweeping view of the waterfront, and fresh seafood. The clam chowder there is the real thing, just fresh hard-shell clams coarsely chopped, some shredded white potato, onion, and a little bacon for seasoning. None of this New England or Manhattan nonsense.

Morehead City is the gateway to the southern Outer Banks communities of Atlantic Beach, Pine Knoll Shores, Indian Beach, Salter Path, and Emerald Isle, all of which are part of North Carolina's Crystal Coast. Head east on state Route 58 in Morehead and you'll cross the Intracoastal Waterway and soon be in Atlantic Beach. If you turn left you'll pass through a few blocks of beach shops, summer homes, the coast guard station, and finally come to Fort Macon State Park, which is on the very eastern tip of the island, overlooking Beaufort Harbor and Shackleford Banks.

Fort Macon was built between 1826 and 1834 to guard the entrance to Beaufort Harbor and has seen use in numerous wars, from the Civil War to World War II. The fort and the surrounding grounds are now North Carolina's most visited state park, with a swimming beach, picnic area, and nature trail.

Route 58 runs the length of the island, past shopping centers, hotels, restaurants, and homes tucked back into groves of live oak. The North Carolina Aquarium at Pine Knoll Shores is next door to the Theodore Roosevelt Natural Area State Park, a good place to spend the better part of a day. A hiking trail runs along an old dune ridge, skirts a salt marsh, and provides a nice open water view. It's a good place to look for birds, especially during the spring and fall migrations.

❖ ❖ ❖

I had birds on my mind when I visited the Crystal Coast, and John Fussell invited me to join an elderhostel tour he was leading at the Trinity Center at Salter Path. John is no ordinary birdwatcher. He's the author of *A Birder's Guide to Coastal North Carolina* (Chapel Hill: University of North Carolina Press, 1994), an exhaustive, 540-page book on finding birds along the Outer Banks and beyond. Janis Williams of the Carteret County tourism office introduced me to him, with the warning that when it comes to birds and birding, he can be very committed and focused—"eat up with it," as

Uncle Buddy used to say. His birding guide doesn't tell you simply which woods to look in, but also which bush to look under once you get to the woods.

We met on a rainy morning at the Trinity Center, a campuslike retreat tucked back in the maritime forest off Route 58. John Fussell was fiftyish, had brown curly hair that was long and thinning, and he smiled often, not nearly as intense as his reputation promised. He joked with the elderhostel members, set up a slide projector in the conference room, and made contingency plans should the rain not abate. At 10 A.M. a slide show on birds of the Outer Banks began, and John discussed birds that the group might spot later in the day: herons, sanderlings, and various waterfowl and seabirds such as northern gannets. After an hour, he was out of slides and the rain was slacking off. We put on our rain slickers and headed out, John in the lead with a tripod-mounted scope over his shoulder.

The Trinity Center is invisible to the tourists zipping by on Route 58. A tiny sign along a modest driveway is the only evidence seen. But if you drive back through the thickets of live oak, you'll find a welcome center, a dining hall, conference rooms, a gift shop, guest housing and dormitory space. The center is operated by the nonprofit Episcopal Diocese of East Carolina and can accommodate up to two hundred people for retreats and conferences. The designers of the center did a commendable job of preserving the maritime forest, the dunes along the oceanfront, and the salt marshes along Bogue Sound. As a result, the center is not only popular for spiritual retreats, but for bird-watching parties as well.

John led us along a wooded path and then into a tunnel, which burrows beneath Route 58. Soon we emerged in daylight and were just behind the primary dunes. A short climb up a wooden stairway took us to the beach. The Trinity Center owns a cross-island strip here, with property reaching from the ocean across the dunes and maritime forest to the marshes along Bogue Sound. With the pedestrian underpass, you can walk from the conference rooms to the beach and to the leeward marshes without experiencing the interruption of automobile traffic.

John set up his tripod and began scanning the ocean, which was gray and frothy after the rain. The first bird we spotted was a gull. "Who can identify this bird?" he asked. "It's a common winter gull here on the Carolina coast."

Several people identified the gull as a ring-billed, and John explained that the ring-bills soon would be moving northward and laughing gulls would be coming north to replace them. Laughing gulls, with their jet black heads and raucous calls, are well known among summertime beach-goers.

And then John spotted another bird beyond the breaking surf. "It's coming right for us," he said. "Large white bird with black wing tips."

Several of us with binoculars picked it up. It was a northern gannet, perhaps the most frequently seen seabird along the coast in winter. Gannets soar like pelicans and dive for fish; when spring approaches they will move northward along the coast to the islands of Maine and Nova Scotia. As if on cue, three of the elderhostel group who had hiked up the beach returned with a dead bird that had been washed ashore by the surf. Another northern gannet, a mature bird with none of the smoky markings of youth, black wing tips and just a bit of orange along the head. John examined it for wounds that might have caused its death and found none. We left the carcass above the surf zone for the crabs to discover.

We saw more gulls, sanderlings, gannets, and common loons, and then John suggested we take a hike to the sound side of the island. Planners and designers did a great job of protecting the maritime forest here, and as a result, visitors can experience the island as it might have been before the Outer Banks became extensively developed. We found many songbirds in the undergrowth, and I made a mental note to return in the spring, when the warblers and other migrants would be making their way through. The cedar thickets would be filled with migrating birds.

From the ocean beach, the path crosses the primary dune, skirts a small pond, and then winds along pine islands and salt marsh to an observation platform on Bogue Sound. The wind had picked up and the sound was frothy with whitecaps. John set up his tripod, quickly spotted common loons and mallards, and then a tri-colored heron passed over. The choppy sound, though, made it difficult to spot distant birds on the water.

John has been birding on the Outer Banks since he was a teen-ager, and he knows the birds of the area thoroughly. Yet, unlike many naturalists, he has a vision that is wide-ranging. He is an expert on birds, but he knows plants as well, having majored in botany at North Carolina State University. On a later walk on a nearby preserve he helped protect from development, he pointed out several rare plants and shrubs. And he has none of the hubris that comes with being an expert. He answers questions thought-fully, and he seems genuinely excited to see a northern gannet passing over the surf, or to see a common loon diving in the break-ers. My guess is the reason he's such a good birder is not simply his experience and depth of knowledge. He seems to enjoy the simple pleasure of being there on the beach, or on the sound, and seeing again for the first time birds he has seen thousands of times before.

Cape Fear

Carolina Gold and a river's currency

More than a century ago, Eagle's Island was one of North Carolina's principal rice-producing regions. It's a low-slung marshy wedge that separates the Brunswick River and Cape Fear River near Wilmington, and if you look closely today you can still see evidence of rice farming. Muddy canals are sliced into the marsh, and at low tide huge pilings and timbers can be seen on the riverbanks where docks once stood. Barges would have come here, loaded the shafts of rice, and taken them to the harbor at Wilmington, where they would have been shipped to processors.

"It was Carolina Gold, a top quality rice," Bouty Baldridge told me. "It brought a premium price on the market." Bouty Baldridge, the Cape Fear river keeper, patrols the waters around Eagle's Island on a regular basis. While his job is to monitor the health of the river, he also is well acquainted with its human history. Rice was one of those fleeting industrial themes that once dominated life on the river. It flourished for years and then died, and now few people remember. I asked him what happened to the rice industry.

"It was a combination of things," Bouty said. "Growing rice in these marshes was labor-intensive, and after the Civil War, when slavery ended, the large plantations had few people to work the fields. Also, mechanization changed rice farming. The equipment couldn't be used in these marshes, because they're too soft. So the Southwest states became leaders in rice production because mechanical harvesting equipment could be used there."

The story of Carolina Gold touches many themes in the history of the Cape Fear region, most notably slavery and the plantation life that dominated the low country southward along the South Carolina and Georgia coast. Although Carolina Gold rice was named for the distinctive color of its husk, it did indeed bring riches to the plantation owners and merchants of the southeast coast. By 1726 the Port of Charleston was exporting 4,500 metric tons of Carolina Gold a year, and the rice had become the standard of quality throughout the world.

Ironically, rice was a relatively new crop in the colonies and had been introduced almost by accident. The first Carolina Gold arrived in Charleston in 1685 when a ship sailing from Madagascar was damaged by a storm off the coast. The captain managed to reach the settlement of Charles Town, downriver of where Wilmington now stands, where he began repairs to his ship. Before leaving, he gave a bushel of seed rice to Dr. Henry Woodward, and from that humble beginning Carolina Gold became a commercial staple on hundreds of coastal plantations from Cape Fear to north Florida. Within fifteen years, Carolina Gold had become the major crop of the southern colonies. In 1700, three hundred tons were shipped to England, and it soon gained a reputation of being the finest rice in the world.

But the reputation of Carolina Gold came at a price. Growing rice required human hands to prepare the soil, plant the crop, harvest and thresh it. Even a small rice plantation of a few hundred acres required as many as three hundred laborers. So Carolina Gold thrived because of two things: The coastal bottomlands of the Carolinas and Georgia had soil that was rich, fertile, and flat, where twice each day tides pushed fresh river waters onto the flood plain. And there were thousands of slaves to wade out in the muck each spring, plant seeds, tend the water control structures, and then to harvest and process the crop in the fall.

As Bouty Baldridge and I were cruising around Eagle's Island, I wondered what life would have been like here in, let's say, 1750, when Carolina Gold was being shipped around the world and making a lot of people rich. At low tide the mud is thick and soft. You couldn't walk on it. In 1750 it probably would have been firmer because it had not seen 250 years of silt and sediment, which has covered the 1750 mud with a tenuous layer of ooze. Still, planting and harvesting a crop here was backbreaking work. The heat and humidity would have been oppressive in the summer, biting insects made life miserable, and there were alligators and poisonous snakes to contend with. When slavery ended, the death knell sounded for the rice plantations; even when offered wages, men would not work the muddy fields.

At the peak of the rice era, the lower Cape Fear region had the largest concentration of slaves in North Carolina. And there is increasing evidence that Africans provided not only the labor to plant and harvest rice but also a thorough knowledge of rice production and preparation. In *Black Rice: The African Origins of Rice Cultivation in the Americas* (Cambridge, MA: Harvard University Press, 2001), Judith A. Carney writes that the origin of rice production in the Carolinas was African, with slaves imported from West Africa's rice region tutoring planters in growing the crop.

Carney says that the sophisticated soil and water management techniques used in rice production were imported from Africa, as was the method of planting the rice: encasing seeds in clay and tamping them into the ground with the foot. African influence also is seen in the practice of milling rice with a mortar and pestle and winnowing it with baskets. Many rice recipes in the Carolinas also reflect an African heritage.

✻ ✻ ✻

The dream of Bouty Baldridge and other conservationists is to see the Eagle's Island area become a national wildlife refuge. This marshy island of cordgrass, reeds, cypress, water oak, and longleaf pine is wild, and hosts abundant wildlife, but it has its human history. And Wilmington, with its restored riverfront, proposed convention center, and shops and restaurants, would provide a perfect complement. The east side of the river would be where people eat, sleep, go to meetings, and learn about the Cape Fear region. The west side would be a refuge, with perhaps a few low-profile floating docks, an observation deck, a place where tourists could gather to watch birds, examine plants, launch canoes, and learn about the area's human history and Carolina Gold.

It could happen. Bouty says the major landowner is a timber company, and timber companies have historically been instrumental in creating many wildlife refuges around the country. Another large tract is protected through a mitigation agreement made when a highway bypass was constructed. And the local soil and water conservation district owns additional land. If it doesn't happen, Bouty worries that the high land will eventually be developed, and the Cape Fear will see more sprawl, more residential housing, more of the development that has surrounded Wilmington along the Route 17 and Route 74 corridors.

As the Cape Fear river keeper, Bouty's job includes monitoring the health of the river, teaching people how to protect it, and acting as an advocate for prudent use of the natural resource. The greatest threats to the lower Cape Fear River, he says, are not the factories that line the north bank, not the containerships and tankers that negotiate the narrow channel, not the dilapidated hulks of warehouses that provide an unpleasant counterpoint to the restored and revived Riverfront Walk of historic Wilmington. The greatest danger, he says, is uncontrolled growth.

"Industries have played a relatively minor role," he says. "Most came in after the Clean Water Act was passed, so they had to meet high standards, and there wasn't a lot of retrofitting that would have been necessary with older industries. They've been pretty good players for the most part."

What worries Bouty are the sprawling shopping centers with acres of asphalt, the residential communities with the chemically enhanced lawns, the apartment complexes, the restaurants, motels, and scores of other businesses that line nearly all the roads in and out of Wilmington, as well as the livestock farms that are proliferating farther upriver. "It's amazing how people just don't realize that the oil that spills on a parking lot, or the fertilizer that's spread on a lawn, will eventually end up in the river. Non–point source pollution is our biggest problem and the most difficult one to address. It's not like you can turn a valve and make it stop."

Bouty, whose curly graying hair spills out from under a wide-brimmed hat, was at the helm of a borrowed twenty-five-foot skiff, looking a bit like Huckleberry Finn, when we explored the Cape Fear. He works on a tight budget. Cape Fear River Watch is housed in a small concrete building under the Route 17 bridge. River Watch is a branch of the national nonprofit organization begun by Robert F. Kennedy Jr. to protect America's waterways. The official River Watch boat belongs to a board member, who occasionally borrows it back for weekend fishing trips. Money comes from memberships, grants, and from small business enterprises, such as a canoe concession at Greenfield Park in Wilmington and nature tourism trips. Bouty depends heavily upon the work of interns and volunteers, not an unusual phenomenon among small nonprofits.

In Wilmington, the Cape Fear is all business. From our skiff, the containerships appear huge; their decks are lined with metal trailers, or containers, that will be lifted by one-hundred-foot cranes onto the beds of waiting trucks, which will fan out across the southeast. It is a neatly choreographed process. A truck driver arrives at the port, unloads his container, loads another, and is back on the road in less than an hour. In the shipping business, time is money. Bouty says it costs $60,000 to $70,000 per day to operate a containership, so efficiency in unloading and loading ships is worth thousands of dollars to the owners.

Wilmington is a working port with a history. It was incorporated in 1739, named after the Englishman Spencer Compton, Earl of Wilmington. Its location at two branches of the Cape Fear River made it a hub for river travel, and in the mid-1800s the river was an outlet for commercial products for more than twenty-eight counties. Barges reached as far as Fayetteville via a series of locks and dams, calling at more than one hundred landings between Fayetteville and Wilmington.

Planters who occupied the Cape Fear river valley exported naval stores such as turpentine, rosin, and tar, which were distilled from longleaf pines that were plentiful in the riverine forests. In turn, manufactured goods were shipped up the Cape Fear to Wilmington, and then were barged to towns and communities upriver. Wilmington grew quickly from 1840 until the Civil War. The Wilmington and Weldon Railroad opened in 1840, opening up a flurry of trading activity. By 1850 Wilmington had become the largest city in North Carolina, and its affluence is reflected today in some of the homes and public buildings that were constructed during the period, such as Thalian Hall, Latimer House, and the Bellamy Mansion.

During the Civil War, Wilmington was protected by Fort Fisher, a fortification that guarded the mouth of the river south of Kure Beach. Wilmington was the final Confederate port to fall to the Union Army, collapsing after a massive naval bombardment of Fort Fisher on January 15, 1865. Following the war, the city was occupied by Union troops and later went through a period of economic depression. The port slowly revived during Reconstruction, with cotton becoming a major export crop. The port grew in the 1900s as more industries moved to the city, and it was not until 1960, when the railroad left town, that Wilmington went into economic decline. The railroad was the area's largest employer, and when those jobs left, the waterfront and the downtown began to deteriorate.

Today, though, much of the restored old downtown is listed in the National Register of Historic Places, and most of the riverfront has been converted from ramshackle warehouses to shops, restaurants, and hotels. The brick warehouse used by the railroad, once an empty shell, now is home to a restaurant and meeting space. Other railroad buildings provide offices and shops, and a Best Western Coach Line Inn has been constructed on the waterfront adjacent to the railroad warehouse. The hotel is new, but the architecture ties in with the brick-and-timber appearance of the old railroad buildings.

When Bouty Baldridge and I cruised by the hotel wharf on an early spring day, students from Cape Fear Community College were taking turns docking a college skiff. Farther along the waterfront, the school's ocean-going research vessel was moored. At waterfront restaurants, people ate lunch on sunny patios, office workers lounged in the sun during breaks, and tourists made their way among the shops and galleries.

"Wilmington is unique in that it is an urban area with a rich history, yet a stone's throw away are square miles of remote wild places," says Baldridge. "It's a balance we need to maintain. The port is vital to the business and industry of the area, but the remote areas are an important asset as well. By protecting these places we're protecting a sustainable resource that will benefit the community for generations. Wilmington is not going to attract tourists who might go to Las Vegas, Atlantic City, or Myrtle Beach. But we have a lot to offer families who want to experience a wild natural area, a beautiful river, a handsome and historic port city."

❋ ❋ ❋

Downstream from Wilmington the Cape Fear widens, flowing through salt marsh, and finally entering the Atlantic at Bald Head Island. It forms the western boundary of the beach peninsula known as Pleasure Island, with resort communities such as Wrightsville Beach, Carolina Beach, and Kure Beach. Near the tip of the peninsula are Fort Fisher, which protected Wilmington during the Civil War, and the North Carolina Aquarium. Near the end of the road, you can catch a ferry over to Southport, a seafood harvesting community on the south side of the river.

The Cape Fear here is a saltwater estuary, with marshes and shallow flats that are a major spawning ground for fish, crabs, shrimp, and shellfish. When the river enters the Atlantic Ocean at Bald Head Island, it will have drained more than nine thousand square miles, covering twenty-six counties, and including more than six thousand miles of rivers and streams. It is a huge watershed, the largest river basin in North Carolina, and the state's only river that flows directly into the ocean.

Wilmington is something of a dividing line on the Cape Fear. Downriver it is a saltwater estuary, but north of the city the river changes character. The cordgrasses give way to cattails, and cypress and sweet gum trees hug the river edge. Bouty Baldridge eased the skiff into the Northeast Cape Fear, one of the major tributaries, and there were men in johnboats fishing with drift nets. The water was still, except for a gentle tidal current, and it was stained the color of café au lait from sediment washed by rain from disturbed land. Farther upriver, away from farms and cleared land, the Northeast Cape Fear flows dark. It is surrounded by miles of forested swamps, whose tannins give the river a color that is glossy black, mirrorlike when the morning sun catches it at an angle.

The Cape Fear river basin is a collection of many rivers and streams that come together like veins, emptying into one common vessel. The river reaches far into the state, all the way to Jordan Lake near Raleigh and Durham in Chatham County, where two white-water Piedmont streams, the Deep and the Haw, come together to form the Cape Fear. From there the river runs south through Harnett County, through the city of Fayetteville, thorough the forests and farmland of Cumberland and Bladen Counties, and finally into Wilmington. A few miles north of Wilmington it is joined by the Black River, which begins in Sampson County where it joins the South River. The Northeast joins the Cape Fear just outside of town. From Wilmington, these rivers flow some thirty miles southward to the salt marshes and sandy beaches of Bald Head.

The Cape Fear is truly a river of many personalities. At its source it is a whitewater stream, rolling over boulders in the Piedmont. And then it becomes a mysterious and dark blackwater stream, flowing through cypress forests filled with colorful songbirds and rare plants. It deepens and widens and becomes an avenue of commerce, helping to define the history and culture of southeastern North Carolina, and it ends as a saltwater estuary, lazily flowing through meadows of cordgrass, meandering through farm fields and forests, finally joining the Atlantic at Bald Head.

The river is ancient and strong, and it also is vulnerable. It is an avenue of commerce, a source of recreation, and a place where one might retreat for a few hours, or a few days, and leave behind the nearness of civilization. Can it continue to fill all of these roles? In the words of Bouty Baldridge, we must find a balance. The key is to use the river, but not to use it up.